How the Stock Market Works

A beginner's guide to investment

The Daily Telegraph

FOURTH EDITION

How the Stock Market Works

A beginner's guide to investment

MICHAEL BECKET

KoganPage

LONDON PHILADELPHIA NEW DELHI

If you speculate on the stock market, you do so at your own risk.

First published in 2002
Second edition, 2004
Third edition 2010
Fourth edition 2012

120 Pentonville Road	1518 Walnut Street, Suite 1100	4737/23 Ansari Road
London N1 9JN	Philadelphia PA 19102	Daryaganj
United Kingdom	USA	New Delhi 110002
www.koganpage.com		India

© Michael Becket, 2002, 2004
© Michael Becket and Yvette Essen, 2010
© Michael Becket, 2012

The right of Michael Becket to be identified as the author of this work has been asserted by him in accordance with the Copyright, Designs and Patents Act 1988.

ISBN 978 0 7494 6402 8

British Library Cataloguing in Publication Data
A CIP record for this book is available from the British Library.

Library of Congress Cataloging-in-Publication Data
Becket, Michael (Michael Ivan H.)
   How the stock market works : a beginner's guide to investment / Michael Becket. – 4th ed.
      p. cm.
   Includes index.
   ISBN 978-0-7494-6402-8
   1. Portfolio management. 2. Investment analysis. 3. Stock exchanges. I. Title.
   HG4529.5.B43 2011
   332.64'2–dc23
                                        2011036258

Typeset by Saxon Graphics Ltd, Derby
Production managed by Jellyfish
Printed and bound in Great Britain by CPI Antony Rowe

Contents

How this book can help

Making money demands effort, whether working for a salary or investing. You get nothing for nothing. Anyone who tells you the stock market is an absolute doddle, and money for old rope, is either a conman or a fool. And the proof of that became very clear with the stock market depressions starting in 2007. But doing a bit of work does not necessarily mean heavy mathematics and several hours every day with the financial press, the internet and company reports – though a bit of all those is vital – but it does mean taking the trouble to learn the language, doing a bit of research and thinking through what it is you really want and what price you are prepared to pay for it. At the very least that learning will put the investor on a more even footing with the people trying to sell.

It has been hard enough earning the money, so this book helps with the little bit extra to make sure the cash is not wasted.

There are few general rules about investment but the most important is very simple: if something or somebody offers a substantially higher profit than you can get elsewhere, there is a risk attached. The world of investment is pretty sophisticated and pretty efficient (in the economists' sense that participants can be fairly well informed), so everything has a price. And the price for higher returns is higher risk. There is nothing wrong in that – Chapter 5 sets out how to decide what your acceptable level is – but the point is it has to be a conscious decision to accept the dangers rather than make a greedy grab for what seems a bargain.

Scepticism is vital but it needs to be helped with something to judge information by, and this book provides that. In the end though, there is no better protection than common sense, asking oneself what is likely, plausible or possible. For instance, why should this man be offering me an infallible way of making a fortune when he could be using it himself without my participation? Why is the share price of this company soaring through the roof when I cannot see any reasonable substance behind it? What does the market know about that company that I do not which makes its shares seem to provide such a high return? What is my feeling about the economy that would justify the way share prices in general are moving?

The stock market is of course not the only avenue of investment. People buy their own homes, organize life assurance and pension policies, and have rainy-day money accessible in banks and building societies. And indeed those foundations should probably precede getting into the stock market, which is generally more volatile and risky.

Shares have had their low moments, for example at the dotcom crash or more recently during the credit crisis, but over any reasonably middle-term view the stock market has provided a better return than most other forms of investment. That, however, is an average and a longish view, so you still have to know what you are doing. That is why this book starts with setting out what the various financial instruments are: shares and other things issued by companies, bonds and gilts, and then derivatives, which are the clever ways of packaging those primary investments. Each has its own character, benefits and drawbacks.

That helps with the decision on where to put your money. At least as important is the timing. That applies whether you are an in-and-out energetic trader or a long-term investor, and Chapter 10 will provide help.

Acknowledgements

I am grateful to Kay Broadbent for her insights and advice, which I occasionally followed. The mistakes of both omission and commission however are mine alone.

I would also like to thank Barclays Capital for the charts from its publication, *Barclays Bank Equity Gilt Study*.

Chapter One
What and why are shares?

Businesses need money to get started, and even more to expand and grow. When setting up, entrepreneurs raise some of this from savings, friends and families, and the rest from banks and venture capitalists. Backers get a receipt for their money which shows that their investment makes them part-owners of the company and so have a share of the business (hence the name). Unlike banks, which provide short-term finance at specified rates that has to be repaid, these investors are not lenders: they are the owners. If there are 100,000 shares issued by the company, someone having 10,000 of them owns a tenth of the business.

That means the managing director and the rest of the board are the shareholders' employees just as much as the shop-floor foreman or the cleaner. Being a shareholder carries all sorts of privileges, including the right to appoint the board and the auditors (see Chapter 11). In return for risking their money, shareholders of successful companies receive dividends. The amount varies with what the company can afford to pay out, which in turn depends on profits.

At some stage the business may need more than those original sources can provide. In addition, there comes a time when some of the original investors want to withdraw their backing, especially if it can be at a profit. The only way to do that would be by selling the shares, which meant finding an interested buyer, which in itself would be far from easy, and then haggling about the price, which would be awkward. A public marketplace was devised for trading them – a stock exchange. Companies 'go public' when they get their shares quoted on the stock exchange to make things easy for investors – a neat little device invented by the Dutch right at the start of the 17th century.

Quoted shares

Once a company gets its shares quoted on the stock exchange there is a continuously updated and generally known market price, which is usually far higher than the level at which the original investors put their money into the fledgling business. In addition, there is a 'liquid' market, meaning there are large numbers of potential or actual traders in the paper, and so holders of the shares have a far greater chance of finding buyers, and people who want to put money into the business have ready access.

Blue chips

All investment carries a risk. Banks can run into trouble and companies can go bust. It has an element of gambling and, as you would expect, the odds vary with what one invests in. The major difference is that the only way to win at true gambling is to own the casino or to be a bookmaker, while in the world of the stock market the chances of a total loss are relatively small and with careful investment the prospects are pretty good.

'It is usually agreed that casinos should, in the public interest, be inaccessible and expensive. And perhaps the same is true of Stock Exchanges', wrote John Maynard Keynes in 1935. He himself made a small fortune on the exchange but is salutary to be reminded of the analogy from time to time and the comparable risks; the term 'blue chip' is an example. The highest value gambling chips in poker were traditionally blue, and the stocks with the highest prestige were reckoned similar. So the companies described as being blue chip are the largest, safest businesses on the stock market.

The companies in the FTSE100 Index, being the hundred biggest companies in the country by stock market valuation, are by definition all blue chips. That is reckoned to make them the safest bets around.

The theory is not unreasonable – large companies are more stable than small ones; they can hire the best managers and fund the biggest research budgets; they have the financial muscle to fight off competition; their very size attracts customers; and the large issued share capital provides a liquid equity market with many small investors and so maintains a steadier price.

The corollary to that is the share price movements should be less violent, giving stability (but providing fewer chances of short-term profits through hopping in and out), and the yield is likely to be lower than on riskier investments. Blue chip shares are, in the traditional phrase, the investment for widows and orphans.

But not invariably: blue chips are safer than a company set up last year by a couple of undergraduates with a brilliant idea, but they are never completely safe. They may be about the most solid there is but they still need to be watched. As an illustration, it is instructive to look back at the Index of the largest companies of, say, the past 30 years and see how few remain. Remember that companies like British Leyland, Rolls-Royce and Polly Peck were all in the Index at one time, and all went bust – though with government help Rolls-Royce did re-emerge as a successful, quoted aero-engine manufacturer. Huge banks were humbled across the world in 2008 as a result of their feckless lending, and even companies that do not completely collapse can fall out of favour, have incompetent managers, and shrink to relative insignificance (such as the British company General Electric, which shrank and then became the private company Telent).

The reason not everyone seeks the safety of blue chip shares is their price – so well known that they are pretty fairly valued, and so the chances of beating the market are vanishingly slim. Being generally multinational, they are also exposed to currency fluctuations.

The next set of companies just below them in market value, the FTSE250, is generally more representative of the British economy, which is closer to home and hence more easily understandable.

Finally, small and new entrepreneurial companies may be more risky but that means they have the potential for faster growth and greater returns – provided of course they do not go bust. It is also worth remembering that even companies like Microsoft, Tesco, Toyota and Siemens were tiny once.

So, not all small companies are dangerous just as not all big ones are safe. This is true even of the multinational darlings that were reckoned deep blue. Just consider the fate of the major American airlines, insurance companies or car makers.

That is why tracker funds have been set up. They buy most of the shares in the index they are tracking and so follow its totality. Trackers reduce the chances of a disaster, mitigate the chances of great capital growth, and should ensure a steady dividend flow.

Returns

Shareholders benefit twice over when a business is doing well: they get dividends as their part of the company's profits, and the value of the shares goes up so that when they sell they get capital appreciation as well. The return on shares over the long term has been substantially better than inflation or the growth in pay and notably better than most other homes for savings. According to data from Credit Suisse, Global Financial Data and Thomson Datastream, the return on US shares between 1904 and 2004 was very nearly 10 per cent per annum, and 8.5 per cent on UK shares.

If the company fails to make a profit shareholders get nothing, and if it goes bust they are at the back of the queue for getting paid. On the other hand, one of the reasons a business is incorporated (rather than being a partnership, say) is that the owners, the shareholders, cannot lose more money than they used to buy the shares. That is in sharp contrast to a partnership, where each partner has unlimited personal liability – they are liable for the debts of the business right down to their last cuff-links or to their last earrings. So even if an incorporated company goes spectacularly broke owing millions of pounds, the creditors cannot come knocking on the shareholders' door.

Stock markets

The language of investment sometimes seems designed to confuse the novice. For instance, shares are traded on the stock exchange, not the share exchange. Nobody really knows why it came to be called the 'stock exchange'. One theory has it that it was on the site of a meat and fish market in the City and the blocks on which those traders cut are called stocks. An alternative theory has it that stocks of the pillory kind used to stand on the site. In the Middle Ages the receipt for tax paid was a tally stick with appropriate notches. It was split in half, with the taxpayer getting the stock and the Exchequer getting the foil or counter-stock. Some have suggested the money from investors was used to buy stocks for the business.

Strictly speaking, in the purists' definition, stocks are really bonds – paper issued with a fixed rate of interest, as opposed to the dividends on shares, which vary with the fortunes of the business. However, in loose conversation 'stocks' is sometimes used as a synonym for 'shares'. Just to confuse things further, Americans call ordinary shares 'common stock'.

Chapter Two
What are bonds and gilts?

The ingenuity of City financiers has produced a wide variety of paper issued by businesses, in addition to ordinary shares.

Bonds

Shareholders are owners of a company by virtue of putting up the cash to run it, but a good business balances the sources of finance with the way it is used, and some of it can come from borrowing. A part of the borrowing may be a bank loan or overdraft, but to pay for major investments most managers reckon it is wiser to borrow long term. For some of this the company issues a different type of paper – in effect a corporate IOU. The generic name for this sort of corporate issue is 'bonds'. They are tradable, long-term debt issues with an undertaking to pay regular interest (normally at a rate fixed at the time of issue) and generally with a specified redemption date when the issuer will buy the paper back. Some have extra security by being backed by some corporate asset, and some are straight unsecured borrowings. Holders of these must receive interest payments whether the company is making a profit or not. The specified dividend rate on bonds is sometimes called the 'coupon', from the days when they came with a long sheet of dated slips that had to be returned to the company to receive the payment.

Here as elsewhere in the book you will come across words such as 'generally', 'usually', 'often' and 'normally'. This is not a cover for ignorance or lack of research but merely an acceptance of the City's ingenuity. Variants of ancient practices are constantly being invented, and novel and clever financial instruments created to meet individual needs. What is described is the norm, but investors should be prepared for occasional eccentricities or variants.

Permanent interest-bearing shares

The world of finance has its own language, with the problem that words are sometimes used in ways that do not tally with their everyday usage. It is not always intended to confuse the layperson – though it frequently has that effect – but specialist functions need specialist descriptions and even financiers have only the language we all use to draw on. One example is the difference between 'permanent' and 'perpetual'. 'Permanent capital' is used as a label for corporate debt. 'Perpetual' means a financial instrument that has no declared end date. So a perpetual callable tier-one note sounds like a sort of debt but is in fact a sort of preference share. On the other hand, a permanent interest-bearing share is not a share at all but for all practical purposes a bond.

Permanent interest-bearing shares (Pibs) are shares issued by building societies that behave like bonds (or subordinated debt). Pibs from the demutualized building societies, including Halifax and Cheltenham & Gloucester, are known as 'perpetual sub bonds'. Like other building society investments (including deposits) they make holders members of the building society.

They pay a fixed rate and have no stated redemption date, though some do have a range of dates when the issuer can (but need not) buy them back, almost always in the distant future. Sometimes, instead of being redeemed they are switched to a floating-rate note.

They cannot be sold back to the society but can be traded on the stock exchange. Not having a compulsory redemption date means the price fluctuates in line with both prevailing interest rates and the perceived soundness of the issuing organization, which makes them more volatile than most other bonds. If the level of interest rates in the economy rises then the price of Pibs will fall. If interest rates rise, their price falls, but if rates fall, capital values rise. There is generally no set investment minimum, though dealers will trade only thousands of them at a time, and stockbrokers' dealing costs make investments of, say, under £1,000 to £1,500 uneconomic.

Pibs provided yields a couple of percentage points above undated gilts. With demutualization and the subsequent collapse of some building societies the yield has been forced higher to offset the risk. The risk is high because if capital ratios fall below specified levels, interest will not be paid to holders and since interest is not cumulative, it is lost for good. Another problem is that holders of Pibs rank below members holding shares (depositors) at a time of collapse, and, as they are classed as capital holders, are not protected by the Financial Services Compensation Scheme, unlike depositors who are protected for up to £85,000. However, building societies are generally low risk.

The good news is there is no stamp duty on buying these investments; interest is paid gross and though interest is taxable they can be sheltered in an ISA (Individual Savings Account); and, for the moment, they are not subject to capital gains tax. It is also worth bearing in mind that building societies, before greed carries them away into demutualization, are run conservatively, so their funds come mainly from savers rather than the much more volatile and unpredictable wholesale money markets. Having no quoted shares, building societies cannot be destabilized by having the share price undermined by specialized bear gamblers selling short (see Glossary).

Loan stocks and debentures

Bonds that have no specified asset to act as security are called 'loan stocks' or 'notes'. These offset the greater risk by paying a higher rate of interest than debentures, which are secured against company assets. In Britain that is commonly a fixed asset but in the United States it is often a floating charge secured on corporate assets in general.

Interest payments (dividends) on these bonds come regularly, irrespective of the state of the company's fortunes. As the rate of interest is fixed at issue, the market price of the paper will go up when interest rates are coming down and vice versa to ensure the yield from investing in the paper is in line with the returns obtainable elsewhere in the money markets. In other words, the investment return from buying bonds at any particular moment is governed more by the prevailing interest rates than by the state of the business issuing them.

The further off the maturity date the greater the volatility in response to interest rate changes because they are less dominated by the prospect of redemption receipts. On the other hand the oscillations are probably much less spectacular than for equities, where the price is governed by a much wider range of economic factors, not just in the economy but in the sector and the company.

Because the return is fixed at issue, once you have bought them you know exactly how much the revenue will be on the particular bonds, assuming the company stays solvent and the security is sound, right up to the point of redemption when the original capital is repaid. Since there is still that lingering worry about whether any specific company will survive, the return is a touch higher than on gilts (bonds issued by the government), which are reckoned to be totally safe. So for a private investor this represents a pretty easy decision: how confident am I that this corporation will survive long enough to go on paying the interest on the bonds, and is any lingering doubt offset by the return being higher than from gilts?

If the issuer defaults on the guaranteed interest payments – which is generally only when the business is in serious danger of collapse – debenture holders can appoint their own receiver to realize the assets that act as their security and so repay them the capital. Unsecured loan stock holders have no such option but still rank ahead of shareholders for the remnants when the company goes bust.

There are variants on the theme. A 'subordinated debenture', as the name implies, comes lower down the pecking order and will be paid at liquidation only after the unsubordinated debenture. Most of the bonds, especially the ones issued by US companies, are rated by Moody's, Standard & Poor's and other agencies with a graded system ranging from AAA for comfortably safe down to D for bonds already in default.

Warrants

Warrants are often issued alongside a loan stock to provide the right to buy ordinary shares, normally over a specified period at a predetermined price, known as the 'exercise' or 'strike' price. They are also issued by some investment trusts. Since the paper therefore has some easily definable value, warrants are traded on the stock market, with the price related to the underlying shares: the value is the market price of the share minus the strike price.

They can gear up an investment. For instance, if the share stands at 100p and the cost of converting the warrants into ordinary shares has been set at 80p, the sensible price for the warrant would be 20p. If the share price now rises to 200p, the right price for the warrant would be 120p (deducting the cost of 80p for converting to shares). As a result, when the share price doubled the warrant price jumped six-fold.

This type of issue is in a way more suited for discussion under the heading of 'derivatives', alongside futures and options in Chapter 3.

Preference shares

Preference shares can be considered a sort of hybrid. They give holders similar rights over a company's affairs as ordinary shares (equities), but commonly holders do not have a vote at meetings; like bonds they get specified payments at predetermined dates. The name spells out their privileged status, since holders are entitled to a dividend whether there is a profit or not, which makes them attractive to investors who want an income. In addition, for some there is a tax benefit to getting a dividend rather than an interest payment. No dividend is allowed to be paid on ordinary shares until the preference holders have had theirs. They rank behind debenture holders and creditors for pay-outs at liquidation and on dividends. If the company is so hard up it cannot afford to pay even the preference dividend, the entitlement is 'rolled up' for issues with cumulative rights and paid in full when the good times return. Holders of preference shares without the cumulative entitlement usually have rights to impose significant restrictions on the company if they do not get their money. Sometimes when no dividend has been paid the holders get some voting rights.

Like ordinary shares they are generally irredeemable, so there is no guaranteed exit other than a sale. If the company folds, holders of preference shares rank behind holders of debt but ahead of the owners of ordinary shares.

There are combinations of various classes of paper, so for instance it is not unknown for preference shares also to have conversion rights attached, which means they can be changed into ordinary shares.

Convertibles

Some preference shares and some corporate bonds are convertible. This means that during their specified lives a regular dividend income is paid to holders, but there is also a fixed date when they can be transformed into ordinary shares – conversion is always at the owner's choice and cannot be forced by the issuer.

Being bonds or preference shares with an embedded call option (see Chapter 3), the value is a mixture of the share price and hence the cost of conversion, and the income they generate.

Gilts

The term is an abbreviation of 'gilt-edged securities'. The suggestion is that of class, distinction and dependability. The implication is that these bonds issued by the British government are safe and reliable. There is some justification for that: the government started borrowing from the City of London in the 16th century, and it has never defaulted on either the interest or the principal repayments of any of its bonds. Although gilts are a form of loan stock not specifically backed by any asset, the country as a whole is assumed to stand behind the issue and therefore default on future gilts is pretty unlikely as well – the risk is reckoned to be effectively zero.

Gilts exist because politicians may think tax revenues are suffering only because the economy is in a brief dip and they want to bridge that short-term deficit, or they dare not court voter disapproval by raising taxes to cover state expenditure. The difference between revenue and expenditure is made up by borrowing – this is the Public Sector Borrowing Requirement or government debt, much discussed by politicians and the financial press. In effect it passes the burden to future generations who pay interest on the paper and eventually redeem it (buy it back at a specified date).

The issues have a fixed rate of interest and a stated redemption date (usually a range of dates to give the government a bit of flexibility) when the Treasury will buy back the paper. The names given to gilts have no significance and are merely to help distinguish one issue from another.

The interest rate set on issue (once again called the 'coupon') is determined by both the prevailing interest rates at the time and who the specific issue is aimed at. The vast majority of the gilts on issue are of this type. In addition there are some index-linked gilts and a couple of irredeemables including the notorious War Loan – people who backed the national effort during the Second World War found the value of their savings eroded to negligible values by inflation – but although this is still on issue it is significant only for economic historians.

There is a long list of gilts being traded with various dates of redemption. For common use these are grouped under the label of 'shorts' for ones with lives of under five years, 'medium-dated' with between five and 15 years to go, and 'longs' with over 15 years to redemption. The government has also been issuing ultra-long gilts with up to 50 years to redemption. On the whole these are probably more aimed at and suitable for investors such as pension funds and insurance companies, which need assets to match the longer lives of pensioners.

In newspaper tables there are sometimes two columns under 'yield'. One is the so-called 'running yield', which is the return you would get at that quoted price, and the other is the 'redemption yield', which calculates not just the stream of interest payments but also the value of holding them to redemption and getting them repaid – always at £100 par (the face value of a security). If the current price of the gilt is below par the redemption yield is higher than the running yield, but if the price is above par (which generally suggests it is a high-interest stock) one will lose some value on redemption so the return is lower.

Since the return is fixed at issue, when the price of a bond like gilts goes up, the yield (the amount you receive as a percentage of the actual cash invested) goes down. Let us assume you buy a gilt with a nominal face value of 100p (yes that is £1, but the stock market generally prefers to think in pennies), and with an interest rate of 10 per cent set at issue. If the current price of that specific gilt is 120p, you would get a yield of 8.3 per cent (10p as a percentage of the 120p paid). If the price of that issue then tumbles and you buy at 80p you could get a yield of 12.5 per cent (10p as a percentage of 80p).

There are other public bonds of only slightly higher risk than gilts. These include bonds issued by local authorities and overseas governments. It is not hard to assess the risk of these. How likely is it that a UK local authority will renege on a bond or become insolvent; how plausible is it that French or German states will be unable to pay their debts in the foreseeable future? On the other hand, there have been concerns in recent years about some sovereign debt of countries with large deficits, and there is indeed a record of such failures as any collector of unredeemed bonds will testify. Chinese governments, Tsarist Russia, US states, Latin American enterprises and so on have all issued beautifully engraved elaborate bonds that are now used to make lampshades or framed decorations for the lavatory, because they were never redeemed. On overseas bonds there is the added uncertainty from currency movements.

As always, and this is an important rule to remember for all investments, the higher the risk the higher the return to compensate for it. So if something looks to be returning fabulously high dividends it must be because it is – or it is seen to be – a fabulously high-risk investment.

In the case of public bonds the slightly higher risk than gilts means local authority and foreign government bonds provide a slightly higher yield, and corporate bonds sometimes slightly higher still, depending on the issuer and guarantor (often a big bank). The differences are generally marginal for the major issuers, seldom much more than 0.3 per cent.

Chapter Three
The complicated world of derivatives

Derivatives are financial instruments that depend on or derive from an underlying security that also determines the price of the derived investment. In other words, these are financial products derived from other financial products. Strictly speaking the term could cover unit and investment trusts and exchange trade funds, as well as a range of sophisticated and complex creations. At their simplest, and not normally allocated to this heading, they are pooled investments.

Pooled investments

The main benefit of devices such as unit or investment trusts is the reduction of risk: you get a spread of investments over a number of companies, which cuts the danger of any one of the companies performing badly or going under. Another advantage is administration by a market professional who may have a better feel for what is a good investment than the average layperson.

Investment trusts

Investment trusts are merely companies like any other quoted on the stock exchange, but their only function is to invest in other companies. They are called 'closed-end funds' because the number of shares on issue is fixed and does not fluctuate no matter how popular or otherwise the fund may be.

A small investor without enough spare cash to buy dozens of shares as a way of spreading risk can buy investment trusts to subcontract that work. A trust puts its money across dozens, possibly hundreds, of companies, so a problem with one can be compensated by boom at another. That does not make them foolproof or certain winners: investment managers after all are only human and can be wrong.

There are also pressures on them to which the private investor is immune. For instance, there is a continual monitoring of their performance so there is no chance to allow an investment prospect the time to mature for a number of years before reaching its full potential if that means in the meantime their figures are substantially below those of their rivals. A private investor on the other hand can afford to be patient and take a long-term view. Similarly, it is only brave managers who decide to stick their necks out and take their own maverick course different from the other funds. They will get praise if they are right and the sack if not. Stick with the same sort of policies as all the others however, and the bonuses will probably keep rolling in for not being notably worse than the industry average.

Some have given up the challenging and unrelenting task of outperforming the market and called themselves 'trackers' – they buy a large collection of the biggest companies' shares and so move with the market as a whole.

Another disadvantage of going for collective investments is the cost. Since investment trusts are quoted on the stock exchange just like any other company, the set of costs is the same as with all share dealings: the cost of the broker (though that can be reduced through a regular savings scheme with the trust management company), the government tax in stamp duty, and the spread between the buying and the selling price, which in smaller trusts can be over 10 per cent. Some can be bought directly from the management company. There are obviously advantages or they would not still be around, much less in such large numbers.

Buying into investment trusts does not entail abandoning all choice. The investor has an enormously wide range of specialists to pick from: there are trusts specializing in the hairier stock markets like Istanbul, Budapest, Manila, Moscow and Caracas (called 'emerging markets'); there are some investing in the countries of the Pacific Rim with some of those concentrating on just Japan; some go for small companies; some gamble on 'recovery' companies (which tend to have a fluctuating success record); some specialize in Europe or the United States; some in an area of technology, and so on. Managers of investment trusts tend on the whole to be more adventurous in their investment policies than unit trusts.

Some are split capital trusts. These have a finite life during which one class of shares gets all the income, and when it is wound up the other class of shares gets the proceeds from selling off the holdings.

As the trusts' shares are quoted, one can tell not only how the share price is doing, but check precisely how they are viewed. It is possible to calculate the value of the quoted company shares a trust owns, except of course for the ones specializing in private companies. Then one can compare asset value with the trust's own share price, and this is published – see Chapter 7. Quite a few will then be seen to stand at a discount to assets (the value of a trust's holdings per share is greater than the market is offering for its own shares), and some at a premium.

One reason many of them are priced lower than their real value is that the major investing institutions tend to avoid them. A huge pension fund or insurance company does not have to subcontract this way of spreading investments, nor does it have to buy the managerial expertise – it can get them in-house. This leaves investment trusts mainly to private investors who are steered more towards unit trusts by their accountants and bank managers. Fashion changes, however, and from time to time the investment trust sector becomes more popular. Buying into one at a hefty discount can provide a decent return – so long as the discount was not prompted by some more fundamental problem with the trust or its management.

Unit trusts

Unit trusts have the same advantage of spreading the individual's risk over a large number of companies to reduce the dangers of picking a loser, and of having the portfolio managed by a full-time professional. As with investment trusts there are specialist unit trusts investing in a variety of sectors or types of company, so one can pick high-income, high capital growth, Pacific Rim, high-technology or other specialized areas.

Instead of the units being quoted on the stock market, as investment trusts are, investors deal directly with the management company. The paper issued has therefore no secondary market – the investor cannot sell it to anyone other than back to the unit trust. The market is viewed from the managers' viewpoint: it sells units at the 'offer' price and buys them back at the lower 'bid' price, to give it a profit from the spread as well as from the management charge. Many of the prices are also published in the better newspapers.

As opposed to investment trusts, these are called 'open-ended funds' because they are merely the pooled resources of all the investors. If more people want to get into a unit trust, it simply issues more paper and invests the money, and so grows to accommodate them. Unlike the price of investment trusts shares, which is set by market demand and can get grossly out of line with the underlying value, the price of units is set strictly by the value of the shares the trust owns.

Tracker funds

Legend has it that blindfolded staff at one US business magazine threw darts at the prices pages of the *Wall Street Journal* and found their selection beat every one of the major fund managers. And indeed the task of having consistently to do better than the market average over long periods of time is so daunting that very few can manage it.

Some managers have given up the unequal struggle of trying to outguess the vagaries of the stock market and call themselves 'tracker funds' (or 'index funds' in the United States). That means they invest in all the big shares (in practice a large enough selection to be representative) and so move with the main stock market index – in the United Kingdom that is usually taken to be the FTSE100. This gives even greater comfort to nervous investors worried about falling behind the economy, and the policy provides correspondingly little excitement, so it is highly suitable for people looking for a home for their savings that in the medium term at least is fairly risk-free – it is still subject to the vagaries of the market as a whole in the short term but on any reasonable time frame should do pretty well.

In fact there are various ways of structuring such a fund. Full replication involves buying every share in the index or sector in appropriate proportions. Stratified sampling buys the biggest companies in the sector plus a sample of the rest, and optimization involves statistical analysis of the share prices in the sector. Just to complicate matters, there is a very large number of things to track. Even if you want to follow the US economy there is the choice of anything from the S&P500, through the Russell 3000 to the Wilshire 5000, which covers 98 per cent of US-based securities.

Open-ended investment companies

These are a sort of half-way house between unit and investment trusts. Like investment trusts they are incorporated companies that issue shares. Like unit trusts the number of shares on issue depends on how much money investors want to put into the fund. When they take their money out and sell the shares back, those shares are cancelled. The acronym OEIC is pronounced 'oik' by investment professionals.

The companies usually contain a number of funds segmented by specialism. This enables investors to pick the sort of area they prefer and to switch from one fund to another with a minimum of administration and cost.

Exchange trade funds

Very like tracker funds, ETFs are baskets of securities generally tracking an index, a market or an asset class. They are dealt on the stock exchange and have no entry or exit fees, but, as they trade like other shares, they attract brokerage charges and do have annual fees of usually under 0.5 per cent. Also like tracker funds they may not buy every share in the index tracked (called 'total replication') but may use some sampling technique that can lead to 'tracking error', ie the performance of the fund does not follow its target completely and this can range from about 0.25 per cent to about 4 per cent, which can outweigh fees and price changes.

The low cost of ETFs has recently attracted a big rise in investment interest, which has in turn brought in a greater variety of products. So much so that the Financial Services Authority has been moved to publish a warning about growing complexity in the products producing higher risk. Another source of problem is the sloppy use of the ETF label – sometimes it is now applied to Exchange Traded Commodities and Exchange Traded Notes which are unsecured assets and hence of substantially greater risk.

Advantages

Everything has a cost. Pooled investments are safer for small investors because they spread risks but, conversely, they cannot soar as a result of finding a spectacular performer. So you pay for the lack of risk by lack of sparkle. They are managed by professionals who must be paid, so the funds charge a fee.

Opting for safety does not mean investors can avoid thought, care or research. Some investment managers are not awfully clever and fail to buy shares that perform better than average. They can be found in the league tables of performance some newspapers and magazines reproduce, as can the funds with startlingly better performance than both the market and other trusts.

Those tables have to be used with caution. The performance statistics look only backwards and one cannot just draw a straight line and expect that level of performance to continue steadily into the future. One trust may have done awfully well, but it may just be the fluke of having been in a sector or area that suddenly became fashionable – retail, Japan, biotechnology, financials, emerging markets, etc. There is also the factor that somebody good at dealing with the financial circumstances of 10 years ago may not be as good at analysing the market of today, much less of tomorrow. On top of that, the chances are that whoever was in charge 10 years ago to take the fund to the top of the league tables will have been poached by a rival company.

The converse holds equally true. A fund may have been handicapped by being committed to investment in Japan at a time when Japan fell out of fashion or hit a rough patch, or in internet stocks when the net lost its glister. Such factors, whether prompted by economic circumstance or fashion, may reverse just as quickly and have the fund at the top of the table. It may also have had a clumsy investment manager who has since been replaced by a star recruited from the competition.

As a vehicle for recurrent investments, or as an additional safeguard against fluctuating markets, many of these organizations have regular savings arrangements. The investor puts in a set amount and the size of the holding bought depends on the prevailing price at the time. This is another version of what professionals call 'pound cost averaging'. It also tends to level the risk of buying all the shares or units when the price is at the top.

One way of mitigating management charges is to get into a US mutual fund, which is much the same thing as a unit trust but has lower charges. The offsetting factor is the exposure to exchange rate risk.

Finally, there is the option of setting up your own pooled investment vehicle. Investment clubs, hugely popular in the United States, are growing up around the United Kingdom. A group of people get together to pool cash for putting into the market. The usual method is to put in a set amount, say £10 a month each, and jointly decide what the best home is for it. This has the advantage of being able to spread investments, to avoid management charges, to have the excitement of direct investment, to provide an excuse for a social occasion, and for the work of research to be spread among the members.

Other derivatives

When people talk of derivatives they are usually not referring to the range of collective investments but mean highly-geared gambles requiring extensive knowledge, continuous attention and deep pockets. Even the professionals got it so spectacularly wrong that the derivatives mire rocked the foundations of the global economy in the 1990s and swallowed some of the world's largest finance houses, banks and insurance companies between 2007 and 2009. If the 'expert' financiers who are paid millions a year can get it so hugely wrong that they bankrupted multibillion pound companies, a small amateur is unlikely to survive long. These shark-infested waters are too dangerous for small or inexperienced investors.

This section therefore is intended as background rather than temptation. Some readers of this book may be gamblers, rich enough to bet on long odds, or grow experienced enough to venture into such treacherous areas. That is the speculative end of derivatives. For others it may also act as a safety net by hedging a perceived risk, or by fixing the price at which to trade within a specific time. But even then one needs a feel for the market.

There is a huge selection of ever more complicated derivatives. They include futures, options and swaps with a growing collection of increasingly exotic and complex instruments. These derivatives are contracts derived from or relying on some other thing of value, an underlying asset or indicator, such as commodities, equities, residential mortgages, commercial property, loans, bonds or other forms of credit, interest rates, energy prices, exchange rates, stock market indices, rates of inflation, weather conditions, or yet more derivatives.

They are nothing new. Thales of Miletus in the 6th century BC was mocked for being a philosopher, an occupation that would keep him poor. To prove them wrong he used his little cash to reserve early all the oil presses for his exclusive use at harvest time. He got them cheap because nobody knew how much demand there would be when the harvest came around. According to Aristotle, 'When the harvest-time came, and many were suddenly wanted all at once, he let them out at any rate which he pleased, and made a quantity of money', showing thinkers could be rich if they tried but their interest lay elsewhere (*Politics* Bk1 Ch11). There is some dispute as to whether this was an options or forward contract but either way it shows derivatives have a long history.

Derivatives are generally analogous to an insurance contract since the principal function is offsetting some impending risk ('hedging', as the financial world calls it) by one side of the contract, and taking on the risk for a fee on the other. In addition there is the straight gamble of taking a punt on the value of something moving in one direction.

Hedging can entail using a futures contract to sell an asset at a specified price on a stated date (such as a commodity, a parcel of bonds or shares, and so on). The individual or institution has access to the asset for a specified amount of time, and then can sell it in the future at a specified price according to the futures contract. This allows the individual or institution the benefit of holding the asset while reducing the risk that the future selling price will deviate unexpectedly from the market's current assessment of the future value of the asset.

Derivatives allow investors to earn large returns from small movements in the underlying asset's price, but, as is usual, by the same token they could lose large amounts if the price moves against them significantly, as was shown by the 2009 need to recapitalize the giant American International Group with $85 billion of debt provided by the US federal government. It had lost more than $18 billion over the preceding three quarters on credit default swaps (CDSs) with more losses in prospect. Orange County in California was bankrupted in 1994 through losing about $1.6 billion in derivatives trading. But the sky really fell in from 2007 onwards when it became clear that most of the major banks had traded in complex derivatives without the slightest understanding of the origin, risk and implications of what they were doing.

There are three main types of derivatives: swaps, futures/forwards, and options, though they can also be combined. For example, the holder of a 'swaption' has the right, but not the obligation, to enter into a swap on or before a specified future date.

Futures/forwards

Futures/forwards are contracts to buy or sell an asset on or before a date at a price specified today. A futures agreement is a standardized contract written by a clearing house and exchange where the contract can be bought and sold; a forward is negotiated for a specific arrangement by the two sides to the deal.

The facility, as with so many derivatives, was originally created as a way of 'hedging' or offloading risk. For instance, a business exporting to the United States can shield itself against currency fluctuations by buying 'forward' currency. That provides the right to have dollars at a specific date at a known exchange rate so it can predict the revenue from its overseas contract. If some shares had to be sold at some known date (say to satisfy a debt) and the investor was nervous that the market might fall in the meantime, it is possible to agree a selling price now.

A gambler decides to buy a futures contract of £1,000 (it almost does not matter what lies behind the derivative – it could be grain, shares, currencies, gilts or chromium). It costs only 10 per cent (called the 'margin' in the trade), so in this case £100. That shows the business is geared up enormously. Three months later the price is up to £1,500 so the lucky person can sell at a £500 profit, which is five times the original stake. It could also happen though that the price drops to £500 and he or she decides to get out before it gets worse. On the same reckoning the loss of £500 is also five times the original money. This shows that, unlike investment in shares or warrants, where the maximum loss is the amount of the purchase money, the possible downside of a futures deal is many times the original investment.

Futures contracts can be sold before the maturity date and the price will depend on the price of the underlying security. If you fail to act in time and sell a contract, the contract can now be rolled over into the next period or the intermediary arranging the contract will close and remit profits or deduct losses.

There is also an 'index future', which is an outright bet similar to backing a horse, with the money being won or lost depending on the level of the index at the time the bet matures. A FTSE100 Index future values a one-point difference between the bet and the Index at £25.

An extension of that is 'spread trading', which is just out and out gambling on some event or trend vaguely connected to the stock market or some financially related event. It could be anything from the level of the FTSE100 Index to the survival of a major company's chief executive in his or her troubled job. If the spread betting company is quoting 4,460 to 4,800 or if the market-makers are quoting 40 to 42 days for the chief executive and somebody thought it would be less than a month, it is possible to 'sell' at 40; while somebody reckoning the chances are better than that and the executive could be there for months to come would 'buy' at 42. Then if the person lasted 47 days before getting the elbow, the buyers would have won by five days and their winnings would depend on how much they staked – at £1,000 a day they would have cleared £5,000. The sellers, however, would have lost by seven days and once again their debt would depend on how much they staked. The market-maker makes a profit on the spread between the two (if running an even book), just as do market-makers in ordinary shares.

The spread betting company, say, offers Brigantine & Fossbender at 361 to 371p. If you think the shares will rise substantially you buy at 371 in units of £10. If you are right and the price then goes to 390p, the shares have appreciated by 19p above your betting price (assuming one unit) and the proceeds are therefore £190. That sounds good until you consider that if the shares had instead dropped to 340p, your losses would be £210. Conversely, if you think the shares will fall, you 'sell' at 361p and the same mathematics applies the other way. If the price remains within the 361 to 371p range nobody wins.

Contract for difference

This is a contract that mirrors precisely dealing in an asset, without any of it actually changing hands. If the price has risen by the end of the stated period the seller pays the buyer the difference in price, and if the price has fallen the buyer pays the seller the difference. CFDs are available in unlisted or listed markets in the United Kingdom, the Netherlands, Germany, Switzerland, Italy, Singapore, South Africa, Australia, Canada, New Zealand, Sweden, France, Ireland, Japan and Spain, but not the United States where they are banned. The asset can be shares, index, commodity, currency, gold, bonds, etc.

The trades do not confer ownership of the underlying asset but involve taking a punt on the price movement, so the contracts offer all the benefits of trading shares without having to own them. Being risky, the contracts are available only to non-private, intermediate customers as defined by the Financial Services Authority.

Investors in CFDs are required to maintain a margin as defined by the brokerage or market-maker, usually from 1 to 30 per cent of the notional value of leading equities. That means investors need only a small proportion of the value of a position to trade and hence they offer exposure to the markets at a small percentage of the cost of owning the actual share. It offers opportunities for large gearing up – 1:100 when trading an index. It allows taking long or short positions, and unlike futures contracts a contract for difference has no fixed expiry date, standardized contract or contract size. As in the underlying market, taking a long position produces a profit if the contract value increases, and a short position benefits if the value falls.

There is a daily financing charge for the long side of the contracts, at an agreed rate linked to LIBOR (see Glossary) or other interest rate, so a delay in closing can be expensive. Traditionally, CFDs are subject to a commission charge on equities that is a percentage of the size of the position for each trade. Alternatively, an investor can opt to trade with a market-maker, foregoing commissions at the expense of a larger bid/offer spread on the instrument. The contracts can hedge against short-term corrective moves, but do not incur the costs and taxes associated with the premature sale of an equity position. As no equities change hands, the contracts are exempt from stamp duty.

Like all highly geared deals, exposure is not limited to the initial investment. The risk can be mitigated through 'stop orders' (guaranteed stop-loss orders cost an additional one-point premium on the position and/or an inflated commission on the trade). A stop-loss can be set to trigger an exit, eg buy at 300p with a stop-loss at 260p. Once the stop-loss is triggered, the CFD provider sells.

The device is convenient if used under around 10 weeks – the point where financing exceeds the financing charge for stocks – while futures are preferred by professionals for indexes and interest rates trading. It is also fairly well hidden – a group of hedge funds linked to BAE Systems acquired more than 15 per cent of Alvis through CFDs without having to warn the regulator.

Acquiring 1,000 Bloggins & Snooks plc shares at 350p each would need £3,500. Using contracts for difference, trading on a 5 per cent margin, you would need only an initial deposit of £175. If you had £175 to invest, and wanted to buy Bloggins & Snooks plc at 350p and sell at 370p, a standard trade would be:

buy: 50 × 350p = £175
sell: 50 × 370p = £185
      profit = £10 or 5.7 per cent.

Using gearing:

buy: 1,000 × 350p = £175 (5 per cent deposit) + £3,325
    (95 per cent borrowed funds)
sell: 1,000 × 370p = £3,700
profit = £200 or 114 per cent.

Although the profit after gearing was far greater, losses are comparably magnified.

Options

Options give the right, but not the obligation, to buy (in the case of a 'call option') or sell (in the case of a 'put option') an asset. That is how they differ from futures, which have an obligation to trade. The price at which the trade takes place, known as the 'strike price', is specified at the start. In European options, the owner has the right to require the sale to take place on (but not before) the maturity date; in US options, the owner can require the sale to take place at any time up to the maturity date.

If, during the time a put option is in force the share price falls significantly, the investor can make a handsome profit by buying the cheaper shares in the market and exercising the option by selling them at the agreed price. Similarly, in reverse, a call option is handy if you think they will rise substantially in the interim. Come the contracted day, however, and the price has moved the wrong way, one can just walk away and opt not to exercise the option. All that has been lost is the margin of option money, which is a lot less painful than if the underlying security had been bought and sold.

This is another way of hedging one's position. Say somebody knows that for some reason they will have to sell a parcel of shares in eight months' time – to fund the down-payment on a house, for instance. But there is a worry the market may slump in the meantime: buying a put option at roughly today's price provides a way of buying protection. If it is one of the 70 or so companies with options traded in the market, there is also the chance to sell the option before expiry since, like most derivatives, options can be traded before maturity.

A company languishing in a troubled sector may look to an astute observer to be about to turn itself round, become a recovery stock, and astonish everyone. But if the observer is also astute enough to have misgivings about such uniquely prescient insight, and worries about committing too much money to the hunch, there is a cheap way in. One simply buys an option to buy.

So if Bathplug & Harbottle shares are standing at 75p, it can cost, say, 6p to establish the right to buy shares at that price at any time over the next three months. If in that time the shares do in fact fulfil the forecast and jump to 120p, the astute investor can buy and immediately sell them at a profit of 39p a share. If the misgivings prove justified and the shares fail to respond or even slump further, only 6p instead of 75p has been lost.

The whole thing works the other way as well, so the suspicion but not total certainty that a company is about to be seriously hammered by the market could prompt someone to buy a put option. That is the right to sell the shares at a specified price, within an agreed set of dates.

These rights have a value as well, related to how the underlying share is performing and how long they have to run, so they can be traded, mostly on the London International Financial Futures and Options Exchange (generally abbreviated to Liffe, pronounced 'life' rather than like the river flowing through Dublin). The traded options market deals in parcels of options for 1,000 shares and at several expiry dates, with some above and some below the prevailing market price for about 70 of the largest companies.

When one buys a security or direct investment, for example 100 shares of South Seas at £5 each, the capital result is linear. So if the price appreciates to £7.50, we have made £250, but if the price depreciates to £2.50 we have lost £250. Buying a one-month call option on South Seas with a strike price of £5 would give the right but not the obligation to buy South Seas at £5 in one month's time. Instead of immediately paying £500 and receiving the stock, it might cost £70 today for this right. If South Seas goes to £7.50 in one month's time, exercising the option by buying the shares at the strike price and selling them would produce a net profit of £180. If the share price had gone to £2.50, the loss would have been restricted to the £70 premium. If during the period of the option the shares soar to £10 the option can be sold for £430. An option provides flexibility.

Warrants

In normal usage a 'warrant' is a sort of guarantee, but in the stock market it is a piece of paper entitling one to buy a specified company's shares at a fixed price. These are equivalents of share options – though generally with the longer life of between three and 10 years – and can therefore be traded. In effect it is a call option issued by a company on its own stock. The company specifies the exercise price and maturity date. The price will be set by a combination of the conversion price and the prevailing price of the actual shares already being traded.

A 'covered warrant' is different, and the 'covered' bit has long been abandoned. It conveys the right to buy or sell an asset (generally a share) at a fixed price (called the 'exercise price') up to a specified date (called the 'expiry date'). It can also be based on a wide variety of other financial assets such as an index like the FTSE100, a basket of shares, a commodity such as gold, silver, currency or oil, or even the UK housing market. As with other derivatives, investors can use it to gear up their speculation or use it as a way of hedging against a market fall or even for tax planning. Unlike 'corporate warrants', which are issued by a company to raise money, a covered warrant is issued by a bank or other financial institution as a pure trading instrument. Covered warrants can either be US warrants (exercised any time before expiry) or European (exercised only on the date specified) but most are simply bought and then sold back to the issuer before expiry. If a warrant is held to expiry, it is bought back for cash automatically, with the issuer paying the difference between the exercise price and the price of the underlying security.

There are a number of issuers offering over 500 warrants and certificates on single shares and indices in the United Kingdom and around the world. They tend to be major global investment banks that have 'bid' (buy) and 'offer' (sell) prices for their warrants during normal market hours in exactly the same way as shares. Investors trade in them through a stockbroker, bank or financial adviser, just as with ordinary shares. Launched in 2002 there are now more than 70 brokers trading. Germany launched its covered warrants market three years earlier in 1989.

A covered warrant costs less than the underlying security; this provides an element of 'gearing' so when the price of the underlying asset moves, the warrant's price moves proportionately further. It is therefore riskier than buying the underlying asset. A relatively small outlay can produce a large economic exposure, which makes warrants volatile, and that means they can produce a large return or lose the complete cost of the warrant price (confusingly called the 'premium') if the underlying security falls below the purchase price (it is 'out of the money'). In addition, warrants have limited lives and their value tends to erode as the expiry date approaches.

Covered warrants can be used to make both upwards and downwards bets on an underlying asset. Buying a 'call' is a bet on an upward movement. Buying a 'put' is a bet on a downward movement. With both kinds of bet the most an investor can lose is the cost of the warrant. Covered warrants are like options but are freely traded and listed on a stock exchange – they are securitized. As a result, they are easy for ordinary private investors to buy and sell through their usual stockbroker.

Swaps

Swaps are contracts to exchange cash flows on or before a specified future date based on the underlying value of currencies/exchange rates, bonds/interest rates, commodities, stocks or other assets.

Interest-rate swaps account for the majority of banks' swap activity, with the fixed-for-floating-rate being most common. In that deal one side agrees to make fixed-rate interest payments in return for floating-rate interest payments from the other, with the interest-rate payment calculations based on a hypothetical amount of principal called the 'notional amount'. Swaps, forward rate agreements and exotic options are almost always agreed privately, unlike exchange-traded derivatives.

As revered investor Warren Buffett warned in his Berkshire Hathaway 2002 annual report, 'We view them as time bombs both for the parties that deal in them and the economic system ... In our view ... derivatives are financial weapons of mass destruction, carrying dangers that, while now latent, are potentially lethal.'

The original purpose of inventing most of them was to reduce somebody's risk – a sort of hedging device. It works in commodities, for instance when a farmer tries to find protection from the potential hazard of a huge harvest (of wheat, oranges, coffee and so on) with the consequent plummeting prices, by agreeing a price earlier and before the size of the harvest is known. If the crop turns out to have been meagre a huge profit may have been forfeited from a big price hike, but the farmer was protected from penury if it had gone the other way.

Chapter Four
Foreign shares

A substantial number of foreign companies are quoted on the London Stock Exchange, especially from Europe (eg Volkswagen, Bank of Ireland, Bayer, Xstrata and Ericsson). In addition there are US companies (eg General Electric and Abbott Laboratories), Chinese (Air China), Japanese (Honda, Kawasaki and Mitsubishi), Taiwanese (Acer), South African (SAB Miller), Chilean (Antofagasta) and Russian (Gazprom). Most of them trade in Britain as well so it is possible to get some idea of the business and see stockbroker analysis of the management and figures. Trading in these is pretty much like investing in a major UK company.

The mergers of European stock markets make it easier to get access to markets in other major countries and their shares, especially as there are a large number of rather good internet-based stockbrokers in Germany, France and Holland.

It is theoretically possible to buy overseas shares through a UK broker – in practice not many of them have offered this service. However, global markets and differential economic performances are producing more opportunities, and the internet and online brokers make it easy. But despite the growth of European traders most of the readily available trade in overseas shares is for US stocks. That looks to change as an ever-growing number of cut-price dealers from Germany and France set up net services in Britain.

As with all such investments, a degree of research and homework are essential. The trouble is that there are added levels of risk in overseas shares. The first is the state of the overseas economy. An investor needs to know whether interest rates are on the verge of change in that country because that might have an immediate effect on share prices, or whether the economy as a whole is about to soar away or is heading for a precipice.

Second, a wise investor gets to know something about the state of a particular sector: one needs to know which is about to be affected by a trade agreement, a reorganization, a spate of mergers and so on.

Third, it is a little harder to keep track of the companies – British newspapers tend not to write about them, stockbrokers do not analyse their figures and one cannot keep an eye on their products and services in the marketplace. There are also local peculiarities, like for instance Swiss shares, which are commonly £5,000 each, with some at over £20,000 for a single share. That makes it harder for a small investor to get a range of these stocks – though to be fair there are ways of buying part of a share.

On top of that there is the exchange rate risk: a comfortable profit from trading in the shares might be completely wiped out by the relative movement of sterling. Finally, there are risks in the way the market itself operates. Regulation in major countries like Australia and the United States is pretty comparable with Britain, but 'emerging' markets can range from the haphazard to the corrupt. As part of that there may also be erratic recording of deals, ownership records may be variable, and controls wayward.

There are people who can cope with all those dangers, and have done very well from US shares, and even from investing in the budding markets of smaller countries. Mostly they know what they are getting into and know something of the circumstances to manage the risk.

For a novice to the stock markets or someone with a relatively small amount of money to play with, it is probably wiser to buy investment or unit trusts with the sort of overseas profile you fancy. There is such a variety on offer, you can decide whether to opt for Japan, the United States or Germany; for the Pacific Rim, western Europe, or developing countries; and even whether to pick specific industrial sectors within these regions. That not only hands over the decision to professionals on which are the good shares, but also spreads the risk. Another choice is to buy the shares of a UK company that does a lot of trade in the favoured area. Those choices also eliminate the foreign exchange consideration since the dealings are in sterling.

Chapter Five
How to pick a share

I started with nothing. I still have most of it.
Jackie Mason, American rabbi and comedian

Anything to do with money is a matter of difficult choices. The savings and investment part also demands a line of careful decisions. First comes the grading of safety and access to spare cash. There is the current account for everyday expenses, followed by the amounts accumulating for predictable larger spending such as holidays, redecorating the home, replacing the car, the children's education, and so on. Then comes the provisions for a safe old age, life assurance, pension and rainy-day reserves. Only when these necessities have been taken care of comes the riskier area of stock market investment. It is not cash you will need to realize at short notice but will supplement income for your old age, say.

Stock market investment is for cash you can spare in the sense that if its value falls it may be disappointing and inconvenient but will not cause serious hardship. It is also for people whose nerves can stand uncertainty – for people who will not lie awake at night fretting about the fluctuations of share prices or get ulcers if the business invested in goes off the boil, or even down the pan. If you can think of it in the sense of an alternative to a flutter on the 3.30 at Sandown, or a punt at a roulette wheel, and can accept reverses with a reasonably philosophical shrug, the stock market may be for you.

That is not quite a fair picture, since if the horse you back fails to win, all your stake is gone. Money in shares has a pretty fair chance of not vanishing completely as most companies stay afloat and to pay dividends to provide some return on the investment. se, unless you were being forced to sell, a drop in share price , _ notional loss while dividends continue to arrive. On top of that, not only are the odds way ahead of other forms of gambling, but the return is better than other forms of investment. Careful research, monitoring and evaluation can reduce risks on the stock market. If the hazards could cause alarm, it does not mean the stock market is closed to you. You can still benefit from the long-term performance of shares by the reduced-risk route of pooled investment vehicles (see Chapter 3). The money is still invested in shares but the dangers of big losses are lessened by spreading the risk.

But that does not end the decision making – on the contrary, it just starts it on a new tack. To sift the right investment from the many thousands available through stock exchanges takes a series of tests and decisions. There are risk/reward calculations and approaches to decide – other people can help by spelling out the options but not take the decisions for you. For instance, some people are prepared to bet at odds of 14.5 million to one against them, which would normally seem insane, but because the cost of taking part in the National Lottery is only £1 and the winnings can run into millions, lots of people are prepared to take a punt.

That shows some of the criteria for decisions. One way of screening the thousands of potential investments is to set your own goals clearly and explicitly. It is not nearly enough to say the aim is to make money out of the stock exchange. The process involves:

- Deciding the acceptable amount of risk. Compared with the return on a safe home for the cash like gilt-edged securities or a deposit account at a building society, is the profit from shares enough to compensate for the risks? How much risk am I prepared to accept, first in general, for investing in shares at all, then in the particular sort of shares to go for – such as accepting that small and new companies are more in danger of failing but do have the potential for a larger percentage growth in both share price and dividend; some companies are seasonal or more reactive to economic fluctuations; overseas shares include an element of currency risk?

FIGURE 5.1   Long-term stock market prices

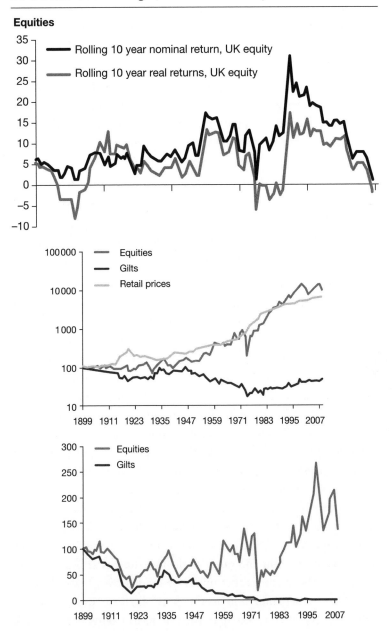

- Setting a time horizon for the investment. Whether the investment is to be short, medium or long term: volatility of share price can be disregarded for the long-term investment and so the shorter-term investments would be more stable businesses.

- Choosing if it is to generate an income or capital growth. The former would send you to companies with a higher yield (the dividend as a percentage of the cash invested in the shares), the latter for companies with lower dividends but the potential for higher corporate growth.

- A host of subsidiary decisions, possibly including ethical considerations, territorial preferences, etc. Some people might be averse to tobacco, arms manufacturers, contraception, dealing with dictators, alcohol, inadequate ecological performance, poor labour relations and so on.

That process should help narrow the field slightly.

Another criterion might be the sort of reward you would need for the admitted risks of investing in shares. Both sides of that equation are subjective – risks vary with the timescale, the choice of investments and the range of holdings; rewards need to be compared with the return from alternative uses of the money such as putting the cash on deposit, into gilts, or into other investments such as property, art and so on. Returns on equities (another term for shares) are usually several percentage points higher than on gilts, which in turn are several points above deposit accounts, but what the real return will be in the future is only an extrapolation – history shows that both absolute and relative values change.

Even that is not the end of it, because there is no reason to insist that the whole investment pot is governed by a single strategy. Or, to put it another way, the effect of even a strong initial strategy can change as the amount and range of the investments grows. The first forays into the stock market might be guided by a low-risk long-term income demand. But as the portfolio extends, people are sometimes prepared to say that, the safe basis having been set, it is fair to try for a higher return by taking on a riskier investment. In addition, as they get more experienced and knowledgeable, some people are tempted to try a little more active trading to benefit from shorter-term fluctuations in particular companies or sectors.

Strategy

Risk

There is no such thing as a risk-free investment. Come to that there is no risk-free life. In investment there is economic cycle risk, company risk, exchange rate risk, income risk, inflation risk, market risk, sector or industry risk, and so on. In this context that usually means capital risk, ie the danger that the share price falls or, worse still, that the company founders. No one share can match all one's preferences, so the policy has to be to balance the spread of shares to match risk needs and then assess each new investment to maintain the balance.

There are risks connected with the quality of the company's management, business area and size. In addition there are vulnerabilities such as great reliance on a managing director (causing major problems if such a key person dies or leaves), or a high portion of business with a few customers (which can be nationalized or go bust). It can also be because the business sector is doing badly through a change in fashion or competing products arriving, or health dangers associated with the product. It can also be because the whole market has fallen flat on its face. The results can be hit by turmoil in the currency markets or interest rates, or the state of the economy. In addition, some shares react more violently to market movements. The degree of this responsiveness is known to professionals by the Greek letter beta, β (see Chapter 6).

Companies with risk factors will probably have higher than average yields. This is called the 'equity risk premium' because it is generally recognized – not just in the stock market – that if you have to carry greater risk you should be rewarded with more money. Higher-risk companies with greater yields are fine for gamblers, or people with a sufficiently diversified portfolio to offset the risk by spreading across other, less dangerous companies and sectors.

Some trades have traditionally been volatile and precarious, and some we can tell from instinct are vulnerable. They may move sharply with fashions, seasons or the economic cycle.

Another good indicator is the way the rest of the world regards the business. There are three useful indications of this: the beta, the price/earnings ratio and the yield, the last two of which are available on the newspaper share prices pages. Beta is a measure of the price volatility, measured against the market as a whole, and is strongly correlated with risk. The P/E is the price of the share divided by the attributable earnings, so a high P/E says the market expects a faster than average growth, and a low one means the general feeling is that the company will languish. In effect the price reflects, or discounts, the expected growth in the dividends the company will pay over the next few years. A very low P/E indicates a lack of market enthusiasm, probably because it considers the business risky.

The yield will show a similar pattern. There is a caveat here, though. Some shares have a low P/E and a high yield not because they are intrinsically dodgy but because they are unfashionable. And this is where the so-called perfect market breaks down and a shrewd investor can get an edge on the professionals. For instance, companies with a small market value were avoided for years for two main reasons: the major investment funds could not fit them into a policy of buying in big chunks of money yet ending up owning only a small percentage of a company; and few analysts bother to look at most of the shares. This neglect meant it was possible for the small investor to find relatively high yields on investments by buying into these companies.

Similarly, if a couple of major companies in a sector – retailing, computers, insurance or whatever – report lower profits, leaner margins and tough times ahead, all the similar companies will be marked down. There is some sense in that, since the chances are that most of them will be affected in a similar way. If one discovers, however, that by good luck, good management, or good products, one company in the disdained sector actually has cash in the bank and is achieving a substantially higher profit margin than most of its competitors (and the figures are reliable and not just window dressing), then it will provide a relatively cheap way in, either for a good income or for capital growth when market sentiment reassesses the whole area of business. In other words, the signals of high risk were misleading or mistaken.

It is a foolhardy investor, however, who relies heavily on this sort of luck or imagines he or she knows better than the market. In general the market is more often right than wrong and the figures really provide a pretty good indication that there is something potentially dodgy. It is sometimes possible to find gold where others see only dross, but do not rely on it.

With investments, as with the rest of life, there are no free rides. Everything has a price. If something has a higher risk, it is likely to offset that with a higher return. What victims always forget when they get caught in something like the Bank of Credit & Commerce International's or Lloyd's of London problems, or a series of frauds like the Nigerian scam or the prime bank paper, is that the corollary of that rule also applies: if there is a higher than expected return there is probably also greater danger. Only very small children and people whose greed overcomes their common sense expect something for nothing in this world.

There is a market in risk. One can hedge against it – take financial measures to limit the extent of risk. Companies hedge their currency exchange exposure on foreign trading by buying currencies forward, and other such devices. An investor can limit losses on a share by buying options.

That in summary is the passive approach, accepting the market's view and making the best of it to suit your personal criteria. Assuming that on a risk continuum of 1 to 10 you are prepared to be cautiously brave by opting for 6 does not mean every share has to be scored as a 6. It can mean a range of really safe 2 with the occasional reckless flutter on something like an 8 or 9.

Each time a buying opportunity comes along, it is worth at least thinking about how it fits into the overall portfolio picture and how far it will move the overall average risk profile. This will have to be done more carefully the longer you hold shares because, as the prices move, the various companies will change their percentage of the portfolio total and their effect on the total risk balance will also alter.

If the long and elaborate process of picking shares seems too hard, or the risk/reward system seems daunting and it all requires more effort than you have to spare, you are not alone. Some of the sharpest investment minds in the United Kingdom and the United States have admitted the chances of being able consistently to pick winners are pretty slim. And in any case, it may be unrewarded effort. The market as a whole, as represented by the FTSE100 Index, does pretty well thank you on any reasonable timescale. Tracker funds that follow the main stock market index can be an answer: the private investor can take a stake in one of those, or be a little more adventurous and go for an investment or unit trust with a broad but selective range of investments.

Defensive stocks

Some companies are reckoned a good bet for volatile or hazardous times. They operate in areas that are relatively immune to economic cycles and include companies dealing in tobacco, as that is a relatively steady market, and supermarkets because people go on buying food. Utility companies also tend to be in demand in bear markets, as people still need, regardless of a recession, water, electricity and gas.

Emerging markets

The label 'emerging markets' is generally applied to small, fledgling stock exchanges in eastern Europe such as Poland, Russia, Hungary or the Czech Republic; in Asia such as Korea, Taiwan and especially India; south America, especially Brazil; and places like Turkey and Israel. Sometimes these markets perform spectacularly well and sometimes they plunge equally spectacularly.

Long or short term

As all the newspapers, magazines and books say, over the long term the stock market has produced a better return than almost any alternative. On the other hand, as Lord Keynes pointed out, in the long term we are all dead.

Over a period of 30, 50 or 100 years, returns from shares outperformed most other investments. They do better than property, antiques, deposit accounts, fine wines, building society savings, and so on. Since 1918 shares in Britain have on average provided a return of 12.2 per cent a year, compared with, for example, 6.1 per cent produced by the gilt-edged securities issued by governments. Those figures are despite the US market falling 87 per cent between September 1929 and July 1932, the UK index dropping 55 per cent in 1974, the steep drop following the hurricane in October 1987, or the plunge from 2007, and the Far East market battering in the 1990s.

Cash in a deposit account would have produced even less than government bonds, probably something under 5.5 per cent. Taking a more recent period, from the end of the Second World War, equities have on the whole (taking into account both income from dividends and capital appreciation) beaten the inflation rate by about 7 per cent or more.

So on average – which is always the important word of warning to bear in mind – shares provide a good long-term home for spare cash. The return on shares is almost always higher than gilts, and certainly so over the long term. This is to compensate for the greater risk: index-linked gilts are guaranteed, while companies are subject to the vagaries of economic circumstances. The resulting difference – the greater return on equities – is therefore called the 'equity-risk premium'. On the assumption you will not have to sell the shares to raise cash at any particular moment, you can afford to take the long view over which shares perform best. Because even normally sensible people forget the dangers, the government has insisted on the apparently obvious wealth warning on all the literature and advertising that the price of shares can go down as well as up.

Another aspect of the decision is whether you want income or capital growth. These are not complete alternatives since any company doing so well that it hands out great dollops of cash in dividends is almost certain to see its share price bound ahead. But not always: even a cursory glance down the prices page of a newspaper will show huge disparities in the yield figures. But if you are aiming for capital appreciation, the shares will be sold to crystallize the profit, while income shares will be retained until they stop producing an adequate flow of cash.

Experienced investors, experts and people prepared to devote time and serious effort deal. It entails bouncing in and out to take advantage of the short-term oscillations of the market. You spot a takeover trend, say among food companies, and get in as the other companies start rising; or you detect a growing fashion for a technology – computers, internet, biotech, etc – and pile in as the boom starts to sweep the shares to unrealistic heights. But this also means you have to watch the market like a hawk and see the sell signals in time to get out with a profit. Such tactics demand more spare money. The proportionately higher costs of spreads, broker's fees and government tax mean you have to deal in larger amounts and achieve bigger share rises to make a profit (see Chapter 8).

One other point – every time one person manages to make a big profit, somebody else misses it. They may not always make a loss but just fail to get the real benefit. What makes you think you will be the winner every time, or spot the real successes and avoid the duffers? Some people do have a talent but not many.

At the more extreme end is the recent upsurge in 'day-trading' (buying and selling within 24 hours), which can be achieved fairly readily over the internet. The figures from the United States, where the fashion started, suggest that fewer than 5 per cent of the people doing it make money.

Ethical investing

The growing insistence on responsible and moral behaviour by companies both towards people and the Earth, means companies with sound ethical policies are more likely to prosper. So such a policy is good not just for the conscience but the wallet.

Personal choice dictates where to draw the line. Companies shunned by some investors have included tobacco, armaments, makers of baby milk for Africa, oil, paper and timber (deforestation), mining, pharmaceuticals (animal testing), alcohol, and so on, to say nothing of specific companies being boycotted because of their policies on pollution, ozone depletion, waste management, personnel, etc. But it can produce confusion if pursued too far. Being opposed to gambling would presumably rule out the National

Lottery, which could preclude all the shops and supermarkets that sell tickets. And how about buying gilts from a government that encourages arms manufacturers, trains soldiers and probably funds research centres that carry out animal experiments?

The ultimate point is that the investor should be able to sleep at night, not just because the money is safe, but because there is no need to worry one is supporting a company that oppresses workers or helps to kill people. On the other hand, it is then only logical that one not only avoids making a profit from the company's success but also stops buying its products.

A useful source of information on this is the Ethical Investment Research Service. It was set up in 1983 by several Quaker and Methodist charities and researches over 1,000 companies plus most collective funds, and keeps a list of fund managers and stock-brokers concentrating on ethical investments. Another is Cantrade Investments.

The economy

Deciding on a share or even a market sector – such as retailers, property developers, engineering manufacturers or financial companies – involves a second level of investigation. It means looking at the economy as a whole and then the way it affects the constituent parts.

Forecasting the economy can be a mug's game. Governments are substantially worse at forecasting than the Met Office. Harold Macmillan complained when he was prime minister that national figures were so out of date it was like driving a car looking only in the rear-view mirror. It has got little better since. Most big companies do some forecasting, the major financial institutions such as banks have substantial economic departments focusing on that, and there are any number of specialist economic or econometric organizations. The projections seldom agree and if any of them is right it is more by luck than by judgement. Fortunately however, the individual investor does not need to get into the sort of complex detail those institutions attempt, and common sense tempered by personal observation will usually help.

Factors that can affect investment tactics include:

- the rate of inflation – both the Retail Prices Index (RPI) and the Consumer Prices Index (CPI);
- the general health of economy – whether it is rising, falling or on the turn;
- the exchange value of the pound – against the euro, dollar, yen or trade-weighted;
- industry trends – eg growth in retail spending, house-building and prices, engineering concerns suffering from exchange rate movements.

On most of these one can get a pretty good feel from reading the newspapers and keeping an eye on what is going on at the local high street estate agents, for example. One can get it wrong, but then so can the pundits holding forth from parliament or on television. And the stock market itself will give a pretty good indication of what the rest of the investment world thinks: if it is falling people expect trouble, if a sector is shunned there is a reason (and it is worth investigating if only to see whether you agree), if share prices are rising optimism abounds (and even then it is worth checking whether you think such euphoria is justified).

Picking shares

Once you have set the ground rules, you need investments to fit them. Warning: almost everyone who has ever had anything to do with the stock market has a theory of how to pick a share. They are similar to addicted gamblers and their sure-fire systems for winning at roulette or horse racing. The bookshops are bulging with pet schemes and private formulae. Those winning methods come in predictable categories. There are the strategic views, which range from in-and-out trading all the time, to the opposite extreme of buy and forget. There is the tactical advice category that shows the infallible way to pick the best bet. It does not take long to demonstrate the fallacy – if there were a certain and predictable scheme for making money everybody would have been using it long since.

That is not a recipe for despair. Although borrowed tactics will not produce infallible opulence, there are some common sense ways of looking at companies and their shares that will increase the chances of success. This is serious stuff however, and an investor who hopes to make money out of the stock market will have to make an effort. Everything has a price, and the cost of making money is usually hard graft. The famously successful Warren Buffett did not get rich by accident or by following a secret trick; he thinks, eats, breathes and sleeps the stock market. He may not be the world's wittiest and most wide-ranging conversationalist, but then you have to ask yourself just how seriously you want to be rich, or even slightly better off.

It cannot be said too often: beware of all advice. Do not reject it out of hand, but just remember nobody gets it right all the time (see Chapter 7). And even the people who do get it right more often than not, seldom know how they do it – their explanations are usually post-hoc rationalization as they struggle to explain just what instinct drove them to buy that or sell the other at just the right time. If by some mischance they really could formulate the trick, they would be very foolish to share the secret with the rest of us and so queer the pitch for themselves.

Judging by the proliferation of such books there is clearly more money to be made from publishing accounts of a wonderful new way of making a fortune on the stock market than from putting the principle to work and buying shares. Why otherwise would all those people be so diligently occupied writing and getting people to compete with them in searching for the routes to fortune, when they could be researching the market and dealing?

The point for an investor is to absorb all information available, but to weigh it carefully and always to test it against common sense. Following someone else's method slavishly will probably not work, but some combination of the methods described in this section should help most people evolve their own way of approaching a challenging but personal task. Here are a few examples to show the diversity of methods and advice available.

One set of investment guidelines has six rules:

1 In funds or sectors go for the ones near the bottom of the league tables. The top performers are usually overpriced or are last year's fashion.

2 Go for shares with high yields, but if they survive that long, sell in a year.

3 Watch what directors do with their shares.

4 Buy companies where at least 3 per cent of the shares are owned by the workforce.

5 Companies spending over 4 per cent of turnover on research tend to do well.

6 Buy after a profit warning if the company is fundamentally sound but going through an unlucky patch.

Even Warren Buffett claims to have a formula (if you can call it that, so wonderfully simple is it), but it is not very obviously helpful to the novice investor. When pressed, his advice was to buy good businesses and hang on to them. Which is about as helpful as the advice for success in business: buy cheap and sell dear. The businessman Richard Koch elaborated: buy companies with a good trading record, specialize, watch profit trends, stick to companies with good business reputations, pick companies that generate lots of cash and produce a high return on capital, risk part of the portfolio on emerging markets, and sell any share that has dropped by at least 8 per cent. T Rowe Price, who launched a fund in the 1950s, advised concentrating on companies with long-term earnings growth records and the chances of continuing that way, which he defined as reaching a new peak at the top of each business cycle. These are in an industry where unit sales and profits are rising, and have good patents, products and management. The US investor Michael O'Higgins reckons you should select the 10 highest-yielding shares in the index, and then pick the five with the lowest share price.

Malcolm Stacey, the author of an investment guide, advises spreading the money among sectors, buying slow but steady risers, and sticking to leaders (including ones in their sector). He also has a system of setting a price differential at which dealing is triggered

– if the filter were set at 10 per cent then every time the share fell 10 per cent off a peak one should sell and start buying again when it came 10 per cent off the bottom.

Many of these people advocating systems have themselves been successful, but note how varied the advice is. So beware of formulae, but be especially wary of fashionable investment gurus.

In clear opposition to all those wonderful systems is the view that any attempt to outperform the average is doomed to failure – it is just not possible. The 'random walk' theory says movements of prices are inherently unpredictable in both size and direction, and as a result any wins or losses are purely a matter of chance. In the long run you will end up even, or at least will have moved with the market as whole.

Another hypothesis that also asserts that trying to outperform the market is a waste of time says the market is efficient in the economists' sense – it incorporates in the share price all the available knowledge. That means everybody has access to all the information about the company, economic prospects and the market, and there are no people with enough financial clout to move the market. As a result, the price of shares already reflects the concerted and probably relatively accurate view of the totality of investors, private and institutional. Since shares have no 'correct' price, runs this hypothesis, and are worth only what somebody is prepared to pay for them, the general consensus view is the right price.

Nice theory, but even the most cursory glance will show the stock market to be anything but random and a long way from being rational. There are anomalies, and not everyone has reacted yet to the information that can be gleaned. Information may be available but not everybody has taken it on board.

In addition, the market does not act in line with the economists' depiction of optimizing behaviour. The swings seem to demonstrate frequent overreaction, amounting at times to hysteria or blind herd stampedes, and it is clear some people do have a shrewder appreciation of what is going on than others. If it were an efficient market, making it therefore impossible consistently to do better than the average, how do you explain people who have actually made themselves – and sometimes their clients – a major fortune?

There are some notable names who have steadily made money and some famous investment managers who have over a long term performed about five to six times better than the market as a whole.

A plain indication that the perfect market is some way off can be gleaned from even the most cursory look at the views of stockbrokers' analysts on company shares – there is little general agreement about the prospective performance of many companies. The price cannot have incorporated all these views because they contradict each other. And as the old saying goes, two views make a market.

The academics are therefore modifying their views and conceding there may be pockets of inefficiency continuing to exist that could provide the sharp analyst with an opportunity. Market practitioners have also pointed out that this sort of rigid academic picture depends on the timescale – in the very short term, movements in prices may seem random and irrational but the longer you extend the period the more logical it becomes.

Fundamental analysis

In deciding what share to buy and when, the first thing to remember is that there is no absolute or correct price. This is a market, so the value is what people are prepared to pay. But that is at any one time. A realistic view is that the stock exchange is quite plainly a very long way from the economists' perfect market with perfect information. But it is a reasonably efficient market so the shrewd analyst can spot companies or sectors that are out of favour or have a greater potential than the market seems to recognize, can anticipate price movements when the new information spreads, and so make an above-average profit. The tacit assumption contradicts the random walk theory as well as trust in the combined wisdom of all traders, and asserts it is possible to calculate the value of a business, and that the share price will eventually tend towards the true value.

This is the province of fundamental analysis. This is the process that:

- evaluates a business and its products;
- examines its published accounts, including return on capital;

- takes a guess at earnings, earnings potential and dividend prospects;
- looks at the economic ambience, such as the rate of inflation, the level of sterling, consumer demand and interest levels;
- watches the market the company is selling in and what its competitors are up to;
- judges the company's management.

A diligent investor can try to keep an eye on advertisements for high-powered jobs in case they show a company about to move into or enlarging an important new area (such as the internet), which could be an insight not available to many. All of that research produces a way of deciding whether the business is fairly valued by the market.

But never forget the price is set by market reaction, so it is pointless to say a company's shares are undervalued. If the market continues to undervalue the business, the shares will become no higher.

The assumption behind doing this work is that the market has developed only a temporary blindness or misjudgement and will in due course come to appreciate true value. So one is aiming to pick winners not yet spotted by others. Assuming the analyst is right and way ahead of the rest of the market, a correction could still take years, during which time the company could be so seriously hampered by its low share price that its business is overtaken by competitors.

There are two additional factors to take into account before acting on such analysis. One is the basis for the current share price and the other is market feel.

Share prices are based more on the future than on the past. That means a price may be lower than the available figures suggest would be just, because the market expects the next set of results to be poor – and of course vice versa. That is often based on a combination of what was in the last corporate announcement and what influential stockbrokers' analysts have been projecting for the figures and have been saying about the state of the company. That is the reason, incidentally, why shares sometimes act paradoxically: falling on the publication of good trading figures or rising after a mediocre result. The market has already factored those numbers into the share price.

and after publication is reassessing the shares in the light of the next set of results. If you think the market has got its expectations wrong it is possible to trade in the hope of a sharp reaction when the true figures come out, if they are in line with your projections. This requires that you are not only right, but that the rest of the market views the new information in the way you have expected.

For instance, a company may be producing pretty comfortable levels of profit and yet its shares fail to respond appropriately. There may be many reasons for that. The company may be too small for the major institutional investors, which dominate the market. Or it might be because the market reckons that further down the road there is trouble looming, or because the price had already reflected just that level of profit, or even because the company may be good but the sector is currently out of favour.

This is where market feel comes in – the result of all that reading of the financial press, listening to the radio, etc, and just good instincts. This is not about being more accurate than others in the market, but being able to anticipate the ways others will see and use new information. Some people just feel there will be an imminent shift in attitudes to a specific company, an industrial sector, or a type of company, but the more you know and the harder you work the luckier you will be.

One way to make such decisions easier is to set them down at the time of purchase. You work out how much the share is undervalued – what would be its right market capitalization, price/earnings ratio, yield, or whatever, considering its sector, performance and prospects? When it passes that level on the way up you watch like a hawk for signs the market realizes it has again overreacted, this time in the upwards direction, and then you must sell at least part of the holding. Never be afraid of missing the boat – it could just be the *Titanic*, as it was for the South Sea bubble in the 18th century, the railway mania in the 1830s, and the dotcom lunacy in 1999, among others.

In 1998–99 any business that had a new web-based idea or which produced software for internet trading, or invested in such enterprises suddenly became the philosopher's stone. Share prices doubled every six weeks, with one going from 230p to £87 in less than a year; companies unknown a few months earlier were suddenly worth hundreds of millions. It was heady stuff and many people got carried away. The boom was clearly unsustainable and triggered an equally exaggerated reaction. It took over a year for more sensible approaches to prevail: the internet is evidently a big business opportunity but will not produce limitless profits overnight. The sensible investors spotted the opportunities early and the very sensible ones realized when the optimism had been overdone, and either sold or at least hugely reduced their holdings.

Bear in mind also that you are not alone in this quest. There are droves of analysts being paid ludicrous amounts of money to help institutions beat the market, plus millions of private investors on the hunt for the end of the same rainbow. As a result, the prices in the main reflect the sum of their expectations both about the company and the market in which it operates. In other words, they set the price not on what it is doing now but what it is likely to be doing over the next couple of years – the price has discounted the future.

Nearly all these calculations are done from published accounts (see Chapter 7). They are filed at Companies House, but most companies will send a copy to prospective investors if asked nicely. Extracting information from the mass of data is a painstaking business requiring application and experience. There is nothing difficult about it, but one has to learn the language of accounting, have an inkling about some of the dodges companies use, and understand the significance of the numbers. The accounts reveal not just what the formulae calculate, but a wealth of other information. Elaborate financial engineering, suggestions of skilful burnishing of results, or careful reallocation of figures are all signs that the business is not all it seems or that the management is a touch flaky. Either way, these are characteristics to avoid.

All this research can yield data of such volumes it buries information. For the private investor the answer is to create a set of personal filters. This can be by sticking to companies with a P/E ratio of no more than five or six, or with a yield at least 10 per cent above the average. It can be by looking at neglected sectors; for example, is it fair that retailing should be under such a cloud; is manufacturing still going through those troubles that made professional investors shun them; are breweries really a better bet than catering companies? In a sense it is being the counter-cyclical investor.

Some people even consider shareholder perks. These are the benefits many companies provide as added inducements: restaurant chains and house builders, clothing retailers and insurance companies, palm-top computer makers to ferry operators, give discounts to shareholders. Those should be a bonus and not a reason for buying.

One then selects from that long list the companies that may appeal for other reasons. The best approach is to combine all of that with the other criteria available, such as a look at the country's economy (some types of company do better on an upturn and some survive downturns better), the shopper's view (see below) and technical analysis (see Chapter 6).

Tracking

All this discussion assumes an investor is trying to do better than the market as a whole. It is not the only strategy. Many individuals and hordes of investment funds reckon the task is too fraught and opt for the safer course of just trying to keep the investments as good as the market as a whole. Since on a longer term the market trend is generally upwards, this is a safe and lower-risk approach.

Shell and recovery stocks

Potentially spectacular changes of fortune could come from shell and recovery companies. They require a specialized form of forecasting. 'Shell' companies have little or no existing business but are clinging to a continued stock market listing. Their purpose is to act as a cheap way for another company to get a stock market quotation. Some sharp managers can move in, raise money to acquire other companies (possibly private), or another business can get onto the exchange by a 'reverse takeover' – the quoted company is legally buying the unquoted but is in reality taken over by the unquoted one's managers and business. By definition it is almost impossible to get much information about such outfits or their prospects.

A 'recovery' stock is of a company that has suffered a poor period and is on the mend, or has acquired a doctor to heal its ills. It could bring rapid returns, but history shows the odds are against you. As Warren Buffett said, 'When a company with a reputation for incompetence meets a new management with a reputation for competence, it is the reputation of the company that is likely to remain intact.'

That is a sobering thought from an acknowledged winner, but it is not always true. Stumbling companies have been rescued from the edge of the abyss by company doctors or revised policies. In addition, though the stock market may show its dislike, the profits could be down for some very good reason: the company has invested a massive amount into research and development for a series of new products that will create huge new markets; it has bought a new business that will extend its own range; it has restructured the company to be more efficient (including expensive redundancies); and so on. It is always worth looking behind facts for causes. There may be the seeds of hope, or Buffett could be right and the loser will sink into oblivion.

The converse does not hold true, as recent years have demonstrated all too clearly. Winners do not hold their top place for ever. J Sainsbury and Marks & Spencer were for a long time revered as the retailers with the magic touch, and it seemed they could do no wrong – until they seemed in the eyes of the market to do everything wrong and their shares tumbled. IBM was at one stage prophesized to eliminate all other computer makers.

By the same token the soar-away success of yesterday seldom lasts till tomorrow. Before getting too misty eyed at the success of a share that has doubled in price in the past three months, just stop and extrapolate – if it goes on like that will the company be able to buy the whole of France and Germany in five years' time? Actually, even without being silly, it is worth considering whether it is reasonable for the business to be comparable with long-established companies such as Unilever or Shell. That creates a sense of perspective and may prompt one to cream off profits and distribute the proceeds to other likely successes.

Bearing all those factors in mind, one can then begin to set the criteria for an investment policy that relies less on hunch and hope and a little more on a realistic appraisal of personal needs and market circumstances.

The shopper's view

Consumers know from personal experience that there are some goods, some shops, and some service companies that really seem good value and helpful, and they keep buying. Other customers may well feel the same way, in which case it could be a good business. And of course the opposite is equally a warning – if you have stopped buying some goods or going to a chain of shops because the goods are shoddy or the value is poor, sooner or later others are likely to spot that as well.

For instance, if shopping at Sainsbury has become expensive and a pain and you are going to Tesco instead, or vice versa, a similar view may strike other shoppers, and eventually the profits and share price will reflect that. Similarly, if you have come across a product or service that seems outstanding as well as providing good value, and the company behind it seems sound and ambitious, it may in due course become a darling of the stock market.

In a wider context, one can spot when a market has abandoned reality and is stoked up on hope and greed. Examples were the dotcom bubble, and the property boom in the 10 years to 2007 when many sane people could see that Gadarene swine were rushing headlong they knew not why, and could sense that things would end in disaster. The shrewd ones listened to instinct, watched sales and prices, listened to early reports of concern and exited with profits.

Losers

There is one outstanding characteristic shown by professionals that seems curiously absent in the amateur investor: the ability to drop losers. Small-time investors appear to have a sentimental attachment to shares they have bought no matter how bombed out the company, or perhaps they just hate to admit making a mistake, which taking a loss would entail. The share price falls from 850p to 55p and they sit and wait for it to creep up again, though any dispassionate view will show it to be heading to something between 20p and hell.

Some investors even go in for 'averaging down' – buying more shares at the lower price to bring down the average cost of the stake. This is on the assumption that the shares are about to recover. But to do this successfully you really do have to be absolutely copper-bottomed certain you are right and the market will soon share your view.

It would probably be more sensible to see if there are better opportunities elsewhere in the market, and shed the loser. One way the big boys keep their policy in check and make such decisions easier and more automatic is by establishing an action point – the stop-loss signal is triggered by a fall of 10 to 15 per cent.

Perks

In addition to the usual benefits of owning shares, such as capital appreciation and dividend income, many companies try to keep shareholders loyal and enthusiastic by providing perks – most of them are merely discounts and therefore entail additional spending by shareholders, which helps profits. For some there is a minimum holding before the perks kick in. Some stockbrokers provide lists.

Chapter Six
Tricks of the professionals

According to market purists there are two basic ways of assessing a company: fundamental and technical analysis. In practice the former is best for showing *which* shares are worth buying and the latter for *when* to buy them.

Fundamental analysis involves evaluating everything about a company. Unfortunately there is too much to know. Ideally you would want to know not only the quality of the product/service, the state of the company's customers and whether a few accounted for a large portion of sales, the competition, the competence of the board and senior management, the condition of finances and the vulnerabilities, the extent to which the business was reliant on a few markets, the economic cycle, exchange rates and labour relations, and so on.

A few of the basic measures and approaches were covered in Chapter 5, but market professionals have a wide range of tools for digging deeper into the circumstances and background of companies. They provide the principal basis for deciding what the underlying value of the company should be, and then seeing how far the market diverges from that.

There is no one simple and obvious way of deciding what a company is worth now, much less how its value is likely to move in the future. All the calculations are helpful sometimes, some most of the time, but none is consistently and reliably able to paint a definitive picture of the business. As different industries have varying payment customs, stock turnover times, capital needs, amounts retained for research and so on, the best way is to check what the norm is for the industry and see how far the company diverges from it. That in turn may take a fair amount of research from people like stockbrokers, trade associations and government.

Another problem is the shifting opinion about which ratio is the most reliable indicator. Obviously, when one factor becomes generally applied as the true measure of a company it distorts the picture. In other words, if dividend cover is taken as the true indication of a company's worth, businesses are ranked by that criterion and a sensible investor would do best to look harder at other factors to see if the market has got its evaluation right.

Many ratios are quite difficult to work out and need a bit of digging to get at the figures. Most of these figures are extracted from the company's annual report and accounts, which should be read in conjunction with the guidance in Chapter 7 on what to look for in those accounts.

The ratios mentioned here are the most common and are generally agreed to be helpful. Experts have a range of other calculations, indicators and ratios they find useful. Those can be handy but only long experience will show what indicators are personally useful, so it will be the more experienced investors who should investigate the serious textbooks on how to calculate and use more sophisticated models of stock market behaviour.

Fundamental analysis

Chapter 5 discussed the reasons for researching a business, its background and circumstances, and how this can benefit an investor. In addition to the general overall feel and cursory trawl through the available figures, there are techniques and calculations used by market professionals that can help pinpoint precisely why a company is better or worse than general sentiment suggests. They are discussed below, in alphabetical order.

Acid test

Sometimes called the 'quick ratio', this can be worked out from the balance sheet. It checks to see just how solvent a company is by having a look at its liquid or readily-realizable assets that could be used to meet short-term liabilities, and then comparing that with its current creditor position.

This means dividing the current assets minus stocks (ie net monetary assets) by the current liabilities. If the result is less than 1 the business could not settle all immediate debts if they were called in and suggests a precarious balance, while 2 is safer. It is also worth checking back in previous accounts to see if there is much movement.

It is a slightly better version of the net current asset and current ratio (see below) because it assumes that not all current assets are equally available to be turned into cash if suddenly needed. For instance, stock and work in progress need time to realize or they will fetch very low prices, and in any case few companies would plan to liquidate all their stock just to pay an overdue bill. So the acid test is reckoned to be a more realistic measure of how easily a company could meet its obligations.

Altman Z-Score

This was developed in 1968 by New York University finance professor Edward Altman to predict the likelihood of a company becoming insolvent within the next two years. The score is a bankruptcy prediction calculation that measures the probability of insolvency through inability to pay debts as they become due. He studied 66 manufacturers with assets then of over $1 million, half of which had gone bust. In one test it predicted 72 per cent of corporate bankruptcies two years before they happened. Z-scores for failing businesses show a consistent downward trend as they approach insolvency.

Altman used five ratios with varying weightings:

1 working capital (current assets – current liabilities)/total assets × 1.2

2 retained earnings/total assets × 1.4

3 earnings before interest and taxes/total assets × 3.3

4 market capitalization/total liabilities × 0.6

5 net sales/total assets × 0.999

The results will be between −4 and +8. Added they produce the Z-score. It can also be thought of as an equation:

$$z\text{-score} = \frac{1.2\,a + 1.4\,b + 3.3\,c + d}{e} + \frac{.6\,f}{g}$$

where:

a = working capital;

b = retained earnings;

c = operating income;

d = sales;

e = total assets;

f = net worth; and

g = total debt.

1.8 or less	a very high probability of insolvency within two years;
1.8 to 2.7	a high probability of insolvency;
2.7 to 3.0	possible insolvency;
3.0 or higher	insolvency is not likely in the next two years.

Consistently low scores each year are more of a concern than a one-off low score.

Asset backing

See Net asset value, below.

Beta

This is one of the few calculations in this chapter not derived from a company's accounts. It is a measure of the share price volatility relative to the rest of the stock market – which is a measure of risk, or at least of getting one's money out when needed. Beta measures how far an individual share moves compared with the market as a whole.

The market is taken to have a beta of 1, so a share with a beta of 1 moves exactly in line with the market as a whole. A beta of 1.6 would move 16 per cent when the market as a whole moves 10 per cent. A high positive beta indicates that a share can be expected to rise faster than average in good times but plunge more steeply in bad. That is characteristic of smaller companies.

Conversely, a share with a beta of less than 1, such as 0.8, rises and falls less than the market as a whole. A share with a negative beta (pretty rare) should move in the opposite direction to the other shares.

Behind this approach there is a sophisticated mathematical philosophy about investor behaviour, stemming from what is called the 'capital asset pricing model'. This suggests that investors can decide on the risk of an individual share, or decide to reduce that risk by diversifying a portfolio. None of that will get rid of the market risk – the shares moving as the whole of the market rises or falls. The measure of that risk is measured by the beta, and an investor would (or should) seek a higher return to compensate for a high-beta share or portfolio.

This approach has the benefit of allowing investors to choose their degree of risk and check that the return is appropriately higher to compensate, and conversely to spot market inefficiencies in shares that have a higher return than would be indicated by their beta risk rating.

Cover

See Dividend cover.

Current ratio

A way of assessing a company's ability to pay bills in the short term is to look at the cash it has and the things that can readily be turned into cash. It is arrived at by the division of current assets by current liabilities. If the result is 1 the two are identical and the company has no spare money. A reassuring figure is more like 1.5 or 2 at least.

On the other hand, a high figure suggests the company may have an unusually large amount of stocks, or it is keeping its assets in cash, which means it earns a larger return on lending than on the business itself or that it cannot find a suitable way of growing its real activity. All are potentially worrying and might suggest the company could make an attractive takeover target for someone in search of cheap cash. It is worth checking if the figure is representative of the industry, however.

Debt collection

Allowing customers credit is expensive because it ties up a company's own capital until the bill has been paid. So it is a mark of good management that debts are collected promptly. One method is to check the average collection time in days. It is calculated by dividing the trade debtors by total sales and multiplying the result by 365.

Debtor turnover measures the number of times debtors are turned over in the year, which is pretty good measure of how efficient the company is in shaking the money out of customers. The calculation is very simple: just divide the figure for sales by the end-year figure for amount of debt.

Debt/equity ratio

See Gearing.

Dividend cover

This shows what proportion of the company's earnings are being paid to shareholders or, to put it another way, a measure of the number of times a company's net of tax dividend is covered by its net profit. If the ratio is 3 or more the company is being extremely conservative; with 2 or more (it could have paid at least double the dividend if it had wanted to) it is reckoned pretty safe; but anything below 1.5 is looking dodgy. At 1 all the earnings are distributed to shareholders, and if the ratio drops below 1 the company is paying out retained surpluses from previous years.

So, if Windowledge plc paid a dividend of 4p a share and its earnings per share were 12p, its dividend would be covered by a very cautious three times. Low level of cover combined with high yield shows the market is nervous about the company's ability to go on paying at this rate. Different industries have different needs for cash, so comparisons should be within the sector.

Dividend yield

This is the amount of dividend per share (usually quoted net of tax) as a percentage of the share price. It gives the return on the investment at the current share price and current rate of payments by the company. As with price/earnings ratios, the calculation can be done on 'historic' figures, which would be based on the most recent dividend figure; or prospective, which would use the forecasts of what the next dividend is likely to be. So if Windowledge paid a dividend of 4p, and its share price is 390p, the yield is a meagre 1 per cent.

That is pretty low in absolute terms, but one needs also to compare it with the yields on other shares in the sector to get the full flavour. As with price/earnings ratios (see below), comparison with competitors gives a good indication of the way a company is regarded by the market. Yield is determined by share price, so if a company is at the bottom end of the generally available yields around, it seems investors expect quite a lot of improvement in the years ahead to bump up that figure.

Conversely, if a yield seems temptingly high the share price is low, perhaps because there is a feeling that the company is heading into trouble and may well cut its dividend, at the very least. Once again, it will take further detective work to see how reasonable those expectations are.

Employee efficiency

This is wages divided by sales times 100, to get a proportion of sales paid out in employee costs. This figure needs very much to be related to the sector since it is obviously nonsense to compare capital-intensive with labour-intensive businesses.

Gearing

A large amount of short-term borrowing leaves a company vulnerable, especially during lean periods. If interest rates rise the business can face a sudden and disastrous drain on its resources. Interest has to be paid on borrowed money whether the company can spare it or not, and if it cannot, creditors failing to get their cash could cause the company to be broken up. Banks can call in overdrafts at will and at times of economic downturn get twitchy enough to do so even at the cost of killing the business. Loans must at some stage be repaid; shares do not have these problems. If times are tough the company can 'pass' (not pay) a dividend payment with impunity. Its share price may suffer but at least the business does not fold.

Some borrowing is pretty well inevitable and borrowing can be a more tax-efficient way of raising capital than issuing shares. The question is not how much it has borrowed but how great those loans are in relation to the value of the business.

The ratio between a company's borrowed money and the money that has been put in by shareholders (which is also called 'equity') is called 'gearing' ('leverage' in the United States). So a high level of gearing – lots of borrowing in relation to the equity – exposes a company in a downturn and is therefore a high-risk strategy. Correspondingly, shareholders of highly geared companies do rather well during upturns.

There are various ways of working out the figures. The simplest is just to take the total borrowings and compare that figure with the total amount of shareholders' funds. That is also the crudest way of evaluating the business. You can refine the calculation of just how great the risk is (gearing is a way of measuring risk) by leaving out the less significant components. For instance, you can exclude short-term debts since these are just the day-to-day business procedures as opposed to the underlying indebtedness. Some people prefer to leave out intangible assets (such as trademarks) as being difficult to dispose of, and sometimes preference shares are excluded from the total of shareholders' funds.

Net asset value

One way of judging a company is by the fail-safe system of seeing what it would be worth if the worst came to the worst and it went bust. The only real way is to check what the value is of all the assets it owns. In practice if the company did go under and had to sell everything it had, the assets would probably not realize the book value because fire sales seldom get best prices.

The net asset value figure, often abbreviated to NAV, can be calculated from the balance sheet by adding up the book value of all a company's assets (including buildings, machinery, cash at the bank, investments, etc). Deduct from that all the liabilities (such as unpaid bills, borrowings, etc) as well as all capital charges such as debentures, loan stocks and preference shares. The remainder is the shareholders' equity in the company, or the net worth of the business. Divide this figure by the number of ordinary shares on issue to get the net asset value per share.

The resulting net asset value per share provides a direct measure of investment trusts because it can be compared precisely with the share price to see whether the trust stands at a discount or premium. In an industrial business, allowing for the fact that the book value of assets is not always what they would fetch in the open market, the result is an indication of just how much solid worth lies behind each share. It is not so much what you have as what you do with it, so the figure is generally only another factor to remember rather than a guide for investment. A company with net assets 20 per cent higher than the share price would make a tempting takeover target. If an offer does come, shareholders can then use this measure as one test of how fair the offer price is.

Net current assets

The calculations so far have been based on total net assets. Some people use a narrower measure – net current assets – which concentrates on cash, things that can readily be turned into cash, and money owed that is likely to be paid in under a year. Net current assets per share that are well above the share price intensify the attractiveness of the business to a takeover predator. There is profit with a minimum concern or doubt because the portions of the business can be sold off in bits without worrying whether long-term assets are worth their book value. So the shares are worth buying because either somebody is going to make the assets work harder – new management or an outside buyer – or the company will go bust, in which case there will be more than enough to pay off creditors and still have money left over to pay shareholders.

Subtracting a company's current liabilities (its debts and unpaid bills) from the current assets, both of which figures are available from the accounts, gives an idea of solvency in the short run. If there is a big surplus the company has lots of spare cash or near-cash to pay debts in the coming year and could therefore get quite a lot of additional credit if needed. A figure close to nothing or, worse still, a deficit, is cause for alarm. See also Current ratio, above.

Price/earnings ratio

Profit is a good place to start when valuing a company. The professionals usually start with comparing profits to the share price. This is the price/earnings ratio, often abbreviated to P/E, which is so widely accepted it is even printed in newspaper share price columns. It measures how many years it would take the company at its current level of earnings to equal the market value (total price of all shares). In effect, this is a measure of how quickly the market thinks the company will grow over the next year or two.

To get the figure, divide the share price by the company's earnings per share. For example, if Windowledge Holdings International has issued 70 million shares and made a profit of £8.4 million, its earnings per share would be 8,400,000/70,000,000, which is 12p (in practice, calculations may be a little more complex since earnings can be defined in different ways). If the share price is 390p then the price/earnings ratio is 390/12, which makes it 32.5. In effect that means it would take 32.5 years of earnings at the current level to pay for the current share price. That is the historic P/E, as it is calculated from the last profit figure; using a forecast of profit for the current year produces the so-called 'forward multiple'.

That 32.5 years is such a long a period that there is obviously something else going on. What is creating such an apparently unrealistic figure is the expectation by investors that the company will not continue making the current level of earnings but is likely to grow fairly rapidly. As a result, the time taken to cover the current share price will probably, in practice, be a lot less than those 32.5 years.

A relatively high P/E therefore indicates the presumption of fast growth. The point to note is the word 'relatively'. At one level it is a comparison with the market as a whole, and at another level it is with other companies in its sector. To get the full flavour of what the P/E indicates one has to take a look at the FTSE All Share Index P/E, as well as the same ratio for the sector in which the company operates (such as utilities, distribution or leisure). That indicates how the company compares, since the ratio is most useful as a *relative* risk indicator.

The P/E therefore indicates what the stock market as whole thinks of the prospects for the company. The obvious next step is to discover the causes of that sentiment. If the P/E is high relative to its sector, is that because the company is fashionable (journalists all keep saying how wonderful the managers are), or is it because it really is about to grow at twice the rate of the other comparable companies? The figure may be prompted by something simple like the rumour of an impending bid for the company.

A low P/E indicates pessimism or lack of interest by other investors. Whether that gloomy view is justified and whether subsequent events will reverse it requires quite a lot of further thought. The P/E being higher or lower than the sector average merely tells you what others think, not whether they are right in their forecasts. Sometimes it may be necessary to disaggregate a disparate group and value operations separately to see if the market has rated them fairly. Life assurers and property companies are particularly tricky to evaluate.

Another point to watch is whether the P/E is historic (uses the last set of published results), which is what the newspaper prices reproduce, or prospective (uses the generally expected level for the current financial year), which is what some brokers' and tipsters' circulars use.

Profit margin

To find the underlying profitability of a company's trading, take trading or operating profit as a percentage of turnover. This is called the 'profit margin'. The figures will vary enormously between trades and sectors.

Quick ratio

See Acid test.

Return on capital employed

The point of a company is to make a surplus, its profit. The reason it borrows or sells shares is to increase that profit. So an important gauge of its success is to see just how well it does it. The point of return on capital employed is that it measures the efficiency with which the company is using its long-term cash.

To get this measure, one divides the trading profit (before exceptional items, interest and tax) by the average capital employed over the period (shareholders' funds plus borrowings) and multiplies the result by 100. A return of 10 per cent is the bare minimum required; 20 per cent is pretty good. A low return on capital shows inefficiency in the way it is using the cash, even if the profit margins are high. The first check is to see whether the percentage is higher than the cost of borrowing. It is instructive to compare the return on cash in the business with other things the company (or indeed its investors) might have done with it.

A common criterion is to see what it would have yielded if put into something really safe, like gilts. If the return from that sort of investment is at least as great as the company's, there is something wrong – there should be a 'risk premium' for putting the money into something more hazardous such as a business venture. If the yield from gilts is at least 5 per cent lower than the return from the company's use of the money, the investment is beginning to seem reasonable. Investors prefer something better than 7 or 8 per cent above the gilt yield.

Return on sales

This is a revealing figure because it gives an indication of profit margins. Start with the pre-tax profit before interest and extraordinary items, then divide that figure by total sales, and multiply the result by 100.

Return per employee

This is another measure of how efficiently a business uses its workers. It is calculated by dividing the operating profit by number of employees.

Return to shareholders

This is another measure that is not derived from the published accounts. It indicates the total performance of an equity over a period such as a year. The figure comes from adding the change in share price (ie the price at the end of the period minus the price at the start), plus the dividends, plus the interest receivable on the dividends, and then taken as a percentage of the price at the start of the period being examined.

For example, a share started the year at 520p and finished the year at 670p. During the year the company paid a 40p dividend as the interim dividend and 50p as the final. The interest rate was about 6 per cent. That would mean the share price benefit was £1.50 and the total dividend was 90p. Interest earned by putting the interim dividend money to work is 1.2p and the assumption is there has not been time to earn interest on the final. So the gain equals £1.50 + 90p + 1.2p = 241.2p, which divided by the 520p opening price is 0.46, so the return is slightly over 46 per cent. Not bad, but it is only a notional profit since it would entail selling the shares to realize it, and there would be a fee paid for doing that, which would reduce the benefit.

Stock turnover

Divide the cost of sales by the stock level at the end of the year.

Value added

This notion was developed in the 1990s to measure how a business has increased the value of the shareholders' investment.

Yield

See Dividend yield.

Technical analysis

The normal contrast to fundamental analysis is 'chartism', which is also called 'technical analysis'. This is concerned exclusively with the movements of share prices in the recent past to forecast how they will move in future. The really dedicated chartist does not even inquire whether the price chart is for houses, airline tickets, gold bars, indices like the FTSE100, or the shares of banks, since all relevant information is assumed to be in the pattern of movements.

This is in complete contrast with fundamental analysis in that it totally ignores the underlying worth of the business. Technical analysis is concerned not with whether the company is efficiently managed but with when the market price is likely to change. It can, however, indicate which share prices are due for a turn – in either direction – and so provide a stimulus for active traders. That means it does not so much indicate which share to buy as when to do so – and this is examined in detail in Chapter 10.

Chapter Seven
Where to find advice and information

Anyone who thinks there is safety in numbers hasn't read the stock market page.

Irene Peter

After a long life I have come to the conclusion that when all the establishment is united it is always wrong.

Harold Macmillan, 1982

Advice

Whose advice can you trust?

At the simplest level, nobody's. Take even the broadest outline advice. Nathan Rothschild said 'The way to make money on the Exchange is to sell too soon.' Another member of the same banking family, Solomon Rothschild agreed: 'One must get into the market as into a cold bath – quick in and quick out.' Timothy Bancroft on the other hand said 'Buy good securities. Put them away. Forget them', which is much the same advice as the Sage of Omaha, Warren Buffett.

As Chapter 5 pointed out, everybody who can find a publisher produces a theory, a system, a formula or an explanation, and a good many bookshops have yards of shelving filled with their infallible advice. Making a major fortune is evidently a doddle.

How about on individual shares though? Think of it this way – what sort of philanthropy could it be that persuades some nice people to make you rich instead of themselves? If journalists really knew which share to buy and when, would they still be hacking away at the computer instead of lolling on some Caribbean beach? How can the authors of books like *Make a Killing on the Stock Exchange*, *How to Pick the Winners*, *Selecting the Soaring Shares* and so on afford to spend all those hours writing when they should be too busy becoming billionaires by trading? Indeed if they were good, why would they share the secret when your buying might inflate the shares they would have wanted to buy?

All advice should be treated with scepticism – even this one. There used to be an old Stock Exchange maxim: 'Where there is a tip there is a tap.' What that meant was that if somebody is persuading you to buy a share there is probably some self-interested motive such as having large amounts of that company's shares on tap.

This is not a defeatist view or insistence that all advice should be rejected, just a recognition that nobody is always right, that some people are unreliable, and that the decision lies with the investor. No excuses, no defences, and no attempts at shuffling off the blame: you choose.

Scepticism should extend to financial advisers. Stockbrokers have an incentive to encourage trading because they make money from commissions on deals. Most of their analysts are clever graduates but few have ever got their fingernails dirty in industry, so although they understand all the corporate ratios, meet the chairmen and finance directors, and sometimes even visit factories, they have little feel for commerce. What they do understand is the stock market, so they have a better feel than the lay investor for how the City, including institutional investors, will react to a company and its performance. Since those are the people who influence share prices, this information is valuable. Its value is about the market, but not about any individual company or about strategy.

Stockbrokers plod through annual reports and issue circulars on companies, but the average small investor does not have access to these circulars, and would probably have little use for them if he or she did. By the time the circulars are printed the professionals have already acted on any insight in them, and there is little evidence that stockbrokers are markedly better prophets than the rest of us. It is not a matter of asking, if you are so clever why are you not rich (because many of them are pretty comfortably off), but once again, would they still be working for wages if they could make amazing fortunes by merely investing?

At least the better newspapers and magazines, unlike stockbrokers' analysts, assess the performance of their share tips at the end of the year. If they do not, you can be pretty sure performance has been dismal. Even that is not a guide though, because personnel change.

There are several reference books, like *REFS, UK Major Companies Handbook* and *UK Smaller Companies Handbook* that provide statistics and facts about business and companies. These are on top of the guides to the Stock Exchange and other investments, plus other explanations of the financial markets.

In summary, there is lots of advice about but little of it is disinterested and even that is not always right. So listen to as many as you can, weigh them against common sense and use them as a factor but not as the final arbiters of an investment decision. Remember that their criteria may be different. As Shaw said, do not do unto others as you would have them do unto you; their tastes may not be the same.

Newspapers

Newspapers, daily and Sunday, devote many pages to business investment and finance. They provide news, comment and advice. On top of that there are many business and investment magazines, ranging from the venerable *Investors Chronicle* to a wide and growing range that includes *Your Money, Money Management, What Investment, Moneywise, Personal Finance, Bloomberg Money, Shares, Money Week* and *Money Observer.* There are also specialist journals such as *Your Pension* and *Which Mortgage* and general business journals like *Fortune, Forbes* and *Business Week.*

Serious newspapers carry company news including reports of results from smaller or less interesting companies, which concentrate on turnover, profit and exceptional items plus directors' pay. They also have columns that concentrate on analysing corporate financial results – eg Questor, Lex and Tempus. These columns do not always make explicit recommendations to buy or sell, but the general message of their comments is usually obvious.

They, like many of the Sunday papers, also reprint advice from stockbrokers. In addition, journalists meet people, sometimes including the management of companies they write about, look at results, talk to brokers and their analysts and trade associations, and discuss business with independent commentators. In the course of this they may come across companies that justify a better rating and are currently being ignored by the market. They may therefore alert investors to shares that are undervalued, and by drawing attention to them may prompt an upward re-rating.

Tips like this can move a share, especially if it is in a tight market – there are not many free shares on issue. The rise is not purely because of buying, but also because market professionals read newspapers too and so anticipate demand by moving up the prices. One consequence is that by the time you have read the buy recommendation, the price at which it was said to have been a bargain can be just a memory.

It may still be worth acting on such recommendations to buy, but it is notable that newspapers are less good at spotting shares that are due to fall. It may be fear of the fierce defamation laws, or that journalists are just more geared to finding winners, but investors should not rely on newspapers for warnings of when to sell a share, although it can be just as important a piece of advice. And nobody is much good at spotting in advance when the market as a whole is about to turn.

The financial pages also carry stories about takeovers and other dramatic events, and have interviews with the top managers. In addition, they carry details of plans, new products, investments, changes of tactics, recruitment of new senior staff, changes at board level, sales of subsidiaries and a host of other indications of how a company is approaching its business. In the course of these articles journalists usually give strong hints about how the management and products of a company are regarded. That gives an added layer of information to the investor.

People have a tendency to say they believe nothing they read in newspapers, but then act as if journalists were omniscient supermen.

Journalists know only what somebody has told them, and though the good ones do conscientiously dig behind the facts and try to interpret and test what they hear, they are fallible like the rest of us. They do, however, mix in the City world, talk to all the people who are directly and indirectly involved and keep an eye on what is going on. Anybody getting into investments would be foolish to lose out on the flood of information that is available. There is daily detail on a wide variety of companies and sectors, discussing the managers, products, performance, deals and prospects. Some of it may be nothing but gossip or a space-filler, but in the reputable press there is often more and better-informed early news about what is happening than comes out of stockbrokers. The more authoritative writers do get read and as a result may move public opinion about a company and hence the share price.

With so many newspaper pages devoted every day to finance and companies, and the large number of magazines concentrating on investment advice, it is hard to see what the tip sheets can add.

Magazines

Specialist magazines provide greater depth of information on a wide range of investments. The *Investors Chronicle* (published by Pearson, which also owns the *Financial Times*) reports a wide range of stock market and economic information and has a speedy summing up of major company results.

Its chartist section requires extensive knowledge of the language and methods of technical analysis; without it one could well be little better off for being told 'the current rally could conceivably take the index through its daily cloud and as high as the black falling trend-line which would likely result in overbought momentum', or references to 'a time-cycle turning-date'. But the pictures make it clearer.

Financial advisers

Advice from newspapers, magazines, radio, television, newsletters and mail shots may be readily available, and some of it free, but investors still have to collect and sort it all, sift the material and test

FIGURE 7.1   (left) and **FIGURE 7.2**   (right)
Information in the *Investors Chronicle*

ELECTRONIC & ELECTRICAL EQUIPMENT
LAIRD GROUP (LRD)

No green shoots at Laird

Last year was a tale of two halves for Laird. Organic growth in the first half was impressive at 19 per cent, but some signs of softening in the third quarter were followed by a dramatic collapse in the final three months of the year and a November profit warning. What's more, profits for the first half of this year are expected to be well below the strong levels seen last year.

Share price 92p

Predictably, there have been a number of measures introduced to reduce costs, including closures of some facilities and a 5,000 reduction in headcount. And while these steps resulted in exceptional costs of £20.3m, annualised savings from this year onward are expected to exceed £15m.

Trading has now been reorganised into three divisions. Handset products, which includes mobile antennae and accounts for 55 per cent of group turnover, saw underlying profits down 12 per cent at £37.4m, while underlying operating profits at the peformance materials division fell 17 per cent to £23.1m. And the story was much the same in the wireless systems division, where profits also fell 17 per cent to £8m. House broker Cazenove is forecasting 2009 adjusted pre-tax profits of £42.5m and EPS of 18.3p (down from £72.4m and 33.1p in 2008).

◉ There is no easy way to avoid the prospect of falling demand as the economic downturn takes its toll. Laird is cutting costs, but paying a dividend uncovered by earnings may leave some potential investors feeling queasy.

High enough

Ord Price: 92p Market Value: £163m
Touch: 91.25-92p 12-Month High: 532p Low: 55p
Dividend Yield: 12.9% PE Ratio: 11
Net Asset Value: 330p* Net Debt: 24%

*Includes intangible assets of £610m or 344p a share

Year to 31 Dec	Turnover (£m)	Pre-tax profit (£m)	Earnings per share (p)	Dividend per share (p)
2007	564	51.5	21.4	11.5**
2008	635	26.5	8.10	11.9
% change	+13	-49	-62	+3

Last IC view: High enough, 67p, 19 Nov 2008   Ex-div: 3 Jun
Payment: 6 Jul   **Excludes 50p special dividend paid in june 2007

F&C Commercial Property

Price: 62p	
NAV: 85.8	
Size of fund: £1.08bn	
Price discount to NAV: 29.49	
Set up date: 18 Mar 05	
Manager Start date: 18 Mar 08	
1-year price performance: -34.59	
3-year price performance: -52.27	
Total expense ratio: 1.00%	
Gearing: 139%	
Yield: 6.612	
Sharpe ratio: -1.12	
More details: fccpt.co.uk	

Geographic breakdown

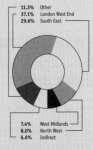

- 11.3% Other
- 37.1% London West End
- 29.6% South East
- 7.4% West Midlands
- 8.0% North West
- 6.6% Indirect

Sector breakdown

Offices	44.2%
Retail	24.8%
Retail warehousing	20.1%
Industrial	9.7%
Shopping centre	1.2%

Source: FT Funds & Datastream

it to see if any of it is worth acting on. This is not only a long and tedious task but the testing is tricky for someone inexperienced in the stock market. In theory, having a professional adviser can improve on that. The stockbroker or adviser can take on board the investor's preferences and needs and so produce tailor-made investment recommendations. Such hand-holding can be valuable, and the good advisers can produce a far better portfolio than an individual who has a living to earn and so cannot spend all day evaluating the options.

Like everything else worth having, it costs money, so its price has to be checked against its value. In addition, no sensible investor hands over the future without asking questions and testing the answers against common sense. Just as an intelligent patient asks the doctor what is wrong and what effects the medicine will have, and a careful client asks the lawyers how the law stands and what the advice is based on, so a shrewd investor should ask financial advisers why they advise a particular course and what assumptions lie behind the recommendation. It is at that point that common sense and personal experience re-enter. If you disagree with the adviser's forecasts of the next six months or five years (and your guess may be as good as anybody's) it is important to say so, so that the portfolio can be adjusted to the satisfaction of both of you.

Such advisers/brokers charge either commission or a flat fee, or a commission on trade (see Chapter 8 on costs and value).

Information

Share prices

Newspapers' share price lists show companies under market sectors. These are allocated by the Stock Exchange and the company will also be a constituent of that part or heading of the FT-Actuaries sector index. It is, however, a bit confusing that not all the newspapers label the sectors in the same way. The choice of sector is not always obvious and some companies feel they are in the wrong group – especially when that becomes unfashionable – so occasionally there is a change of allocation by the Stock Exchange authorities, though that happens mostly when the company itself has altered the emphasis of its work.

There are over 3,000 companies quoted on the London Stock Exchange, some with several types of issues, plus the Alternative Investment Market (Aim), Techmark, and Plus-Markets. The majority of companies are traded infrequently, with the greatest volume of interest and trade being in the hundred largest companies by market value. Those are the components of the FTSE100 Share Index (called the 'Footsie'), which is the main indicator of stock market trends. The major companies in it make them important in the investment strategy of the large financial institutions. The concentration of institutional interest is shown most clearly at the time of the quarterly review when the market values of companies on a specific date are reviewed and there is a change in the composition of the Index. The moment a company drops out of the Index its shares may take a sudden fall, sometimes by as much as 5 per cent, while the new member of the elite sometimes sees a sudden additional jump. Some tracker funds and investors see the way things are going and deal in the shares before the company gains or loses its status in a particular index, which can mean the shares do not move much. Another index review worth watching is the Morgan Stanley Capital International (MSCI). While the focus is global, UK companies do regularly move in or out of the index, which can lead to moves in share prices.

Below that top level is the second tier, made up of the next 250 companies measured once again by market capitalization – that is, in both these categories it is not turnover, profit, asset value or any other measure that counts, merely the aggregate value of issued shares. All the 350 largest companies are in the lists of the serious newspapers' prices pages, which also contain several hundred other companies. But none of the papers has the space to show all the securities available. Even the *Financial Times,* which devotes more pages than the others to share prices, can show only part of the list actually quoted. Newspaper lists are not necessarily a signal of significance – most of the companies pay to have their shares listed in the prices pages.

Newspapers display a range of information apart from the latest share price, including how the share price moved from the closing of the previous day, and so on.

Figure 7.3 is an example of *The Daily Telegraph* prices page. It shows in the third column the company name, sometimes in abbreviated form, and if the shares were not issued in sterling, the currency is also given. Almost always what is quoted is the ordinary share (called 'common stock' in the United States), but some companies issue other quoted paper, such as irredeemable preference stock, convertibles, warrants and so on, and these are normally listed underneath. Sometimes there are additional symbols. For instance, in the *Financial Times*:

$, €, ¥	a currency symbol next to the company name says the shares are not priced in sterling;
*	high and low share prices have been adjusted for capital changes;
†	interim dividend increased or resumed;
‡	interim dividend since reduced, passed or deferred;
#	dividend price at the time the dealing in the share was suspended;
c	cents
d	fair value net asset value is more than 3% different from the par value NAV;
q	undated
P	dividend adjusted for consolidation or split in the shares;
xd	the recently-declared dividend will be retained by the current holder of the share;
xr	the same for rights issue – the buyer will not be entitled to subscribe to new shares;
xR	buyer does not get the scrip issue;
xa	ex-all – several of those rights remain with the current holder;
	there no longer seems to be a symbol for the most traded stock.

FIGURE 7.3 *Daily Telegraph* prices page entry

| | 52 week | | | | + or | | | |
	High	Low	Stock	Price	−		Yld	P/E

GOVERNMENT SECURITIES

52 week			+ or	Yield	
High	Low	Stock	Price −	Flat	Rm@
£s	%	£s			
104.98	100.39	Treas. 5¾ 09 .	102.54+0.02	5.61	0.60
109.90	101.75	Treas. 6¼%10 .	107.38−0.22	5.82	1.14
118.37	109.51	Conv 9%2011	114.94−0.39	7.83	1.70
116.94	106.76	Treas7¾%12'15 .	114.00...	7.02	2.24
109.75	98.55	Treas 5%12	107.06−0.51	4.67	2.33
125.58	111.45	Treas 8%13	120.19−0.74	6.66	2.96
115.08	98.24	Treas 5%14	110.25...	4.54	2.88
114.78	96.73	Treas 4¾%15..	109.89−0.43	4.32	3.00
135.27	115.47	Treas 8%15	129.86−0.35	6.16	2.92
145.62	123.69	Treas 8¾%17..	138.07+0.23	6.34	3.40
148.70	124.69	Treas 8%21	139.57+0.80	5.73	3.85
117.56	91.73	Treas 5%25	107.96+0.94	4.63	4.30

ELECTRICALS ▼2.08%

High	Low	Stock	Price	+ or −	Yld	P/E
197½	87	Acal	110	...	6.4	9.9
269½	111¾	Chloride♦	150	−1¼	3.1	13.2
182¼	100¼	Dialight	121	+1	5.0	10.7
213½	143¼	Halma♦	170¾	−7	4.3	12.5
322	122	**Invensys**	231	−3½	0.6	16.6
500	54½	Laird Gp	138¼	−13¾	7.8	5.5
235	67¾	Morgan Cru♦	102¾	*+½	6.8	4.4
250¾	107	Oxford Inst	148	+4½	5.8	11.2
210¼	10¼	Raymarine	18	−¼	18.5	1.1
881	248½	Renishaw	427	−8¼	5.8	9.4
128½	19¼	TT Electronic .	28½	+1	13.4	3.0
248	115¾	XP Power	207½	−3½	8.2	6.5
211	39	Xaar	80	·»...	3.1	12.9

The *Daily Telegraph* share price codes are:

bold type	FTSE100 index shares;
♦	FTSE250 index shares;
*	ex-dividend;
†	ex-scrip;
§	ex-rights;
‡	ex-all;
#	share dealings have been suspended;
A	report and accounts are not ready.

The fourth column gives the price at which the shares stood at close of trading the previous night or the last trading day. Anybody who has bought holiday money knows the price of buying is always higher than the price at which you can sell, and that difference is called the 'spread'. The published price is the average of the two, so no investor can hope to buy at the price or sell at it, even if the market had not moved by the time the newspaper arrives through the letterbox. If trading in the shares has been suspended – say because the company is being reorganized, or there are questions about the figures, or because it is subject to a takeover – the price listed is the last one before suspension, with # next to it.

FIGURE 7.4   *Financial Times* prices page entry

	Notes	Price	Chng	52 Week High	Low	Yld	P/E	Vol '000s
Tech – Software & Services								
Alterian.....q		104.50	+2	134.50	46.50	–	8.9	36
Anite.........‡		39	+1	44.70	23.10	2.3	14.2	402
AVEVA.......q		727	+6	£16.40	449.50	1.3	11.7	283
Computcnt..		206.75xd	+2.75	213.75	66.50	4	7.6	203
Dimensn.....		56	+0.50	59.50	22.25	1.9	12.8	7,047
DRS Data....		16	+1.50	22	10.50	1.9	–	–
Elecdata.....		42.50	+1	63.99	37	6.4	19.2	–
Invensys..q		231	–3.50	321.50	115.33	0.6	14.2	4,269
Kewill.......†		74	+0.50	97	33.50	1.1	26.4	48
Kofax.........		137	+1.50	217	101	1.8	32.6	9
Logica........		70.75	–1.75	145.50	57.50	4.2	21.6	4,661
MicroFoc...†		374	–11.50	454.25	186.25	2.6	18.7	282
Microgen....		55.50	–	57	35.50	3.8	10.6	–
Misys........‡		158.75	–1.75	180.25	78	3.1	14.8	783
Morse.......‡		12.25	–	54.50	4.51	10.6	42.7	94
NCC Gp.....†		352.50	+2.50	420	265	2.2	16.4	2
PhoenixIT..q		193	+4.50	326.50	127	3.3	11	12
RM...........†		165xd	–1	211.52	137	3.6	13.5	127
Sage........†		182.30xd	–1.40	227	143.50	4	13.3	6,133
SDL...........		340.50	+5.50	395	187	–	17.8	162
Telecity......		293.75	+0.50	318	130	–	22.6	114
TriadGp......		32.50	–	34.50	10.50	–	–	–

With shares the spread will depend on a range of factors that affect the dealer's risk. One is what the market calls 'liquidity': how many shares there are available and how many people are prepared to trade in them. A good measure as far as the stock market is concerned is how much the price moves when you try to trade. Try to buy shares in a company with few on issue, and most of those locked up by holders not prepared to be tempted out by a small rise in the value, and the price will suddenly bounce.

Massive companies like British Telecom, Vodafone, etc have millions of shares on issue and there is always somebody in the market wanting to deal in them. By contrast, a relatively small business with a market capitalization of £10 million, of which the manager and family own half and directors own another quarter, with most of the rest held by the initial investors, are very difficult to trade in. Its size means few people have heard about the business, so not many want to deal in the shares, and even if they did want to it could be quite tricky to find a counterparty. So the first will have a relatively narrow spread because the more trade there is in a share the more confident the dealer is in getting shot of any, while the latter will probably have a frighteningly wide spread. The width of the spread also depends on the state of the market. In wildly fluctuating shares, market-makers are loath to stick their necks out and they carefully widen the spread. So the middle market price is just an indication of the actual rate the shares will fetch in a real deal.

People who deal over the telephone can ask the broker, who will look at the Stock Exchange screen showing all the people dealing in the shares and their prices. The broker can specify exactly what the price is then and, if the agreement is swift, may be able to deal at that price. An alternative is to get access to the prices pages via the internet, and check the prices for oneself.

The fifth column in the *Daily Telegraph* shows the price change from the previous day's closing level, also at the mid-market price. The next two columns show the highs and lows the share price has reached over the previous year overall. That will indicate whether the share is near its maximum or minimum. So if the share price is currently 127p and the high and lows are 478p and 123p, you can immediately tell that the price is very near the bottom level it has reached in the past year.

Volume of trade in the final column of the *Financial Times* shows how many thousands of shares changed hands on the previous trading day. The figure is the total of equities bought and sold – in other words, there is double counting. The figure shows the level of interest in the company's shares and is an indication of the liquidity in the market. It is salutary to see how many were not dealt in at all. Some newspapers print a separate table of the previous day's most highly-traded shares.

Yield is the percentage return you get if investing at the share price listed in the table and at the current rate of dividends. The formula is: multiply the annual gross dividend by 100, and then divide by the share's market price. So if the shares cost 200p and the latest year's dividend was 14p, the yield is 7 per cent. This is normally reported gross, ie before tax has been deducted, though almost everybody gets the dividend cheques net and the tax is not reclaimable.

The *Daily Telegraph* prices pages print the letter 'b' to indicate the interim dividend has been raised; 'c' means the interim dividend has been reduced or it has been omitted altogether.

The P/E stands for price/earnings ratio, and is probably the best known method of assessing equities. It is calculated by comparing the current share price with the level of earnings per share (found in the company's accounts).

The company's accounts may say something like, 'attributable to ordinary shareholders £850,000' and at the bottom of the profit and loss table it will say something like 'earnings on each of the 10 million shares on issue 8½p'. To get the P/E ratio you divide this 8½ into the prevailing market price of the shares. If those stand at, say, 170p, then 170/8½ = 20. If the share price halves to 85p the P/E ratio would be 10, and if the shares shot up to 255p the P/E would be 30.

One can then inspect the other companies in the same industry sector listed in the newspaper and see how they compare. If most of the companies are on a P/E of between 12 and 16 and one of the companies is on 25, either the market knows great things are on the way from it, or the shares are grossly overpriced. Conversely, if all the sector is on a P/E of 18 to 20 but one of the companies is on 4, either the market knows there is some nasty news on the way from the management or they are wrong and the shares are grossly underpriced.

Investment trusts

Instead of price/earnings ratios, the column for investment trusts shows 'NAV', which stands for net asset value. That is a calculation of the investment trust's holdings as a value per share. Like the share price, it is quoted in pence. The *Financial Times* also has a column showing 'Dis or Pm (–)'. That is a calculation of the difference between the net asset value and the actual price of the share – 'Dis' means the shares are at a discount as the price is below the asset value; 'Pm' means the shares are at a premium to the underlying value of the investments. Perversely and confusingly, a discount is shown as a positive figure, while a premium is shown with a minus sign.

The Association of Investment Companies produces a monthly booklet on the prices and detailed other figures of its members.

Gilts

There are also price tables for gilts – government-issued securities. These are usually split into short, medium and long-dated. There are also the two undated ones, and index-linked stocks. Foreign governments also issue bonds that are obtainable in Britain and are quoted sometimes with a lower yield than native varieties. (See page 81 for the *Daily Telegraph* prices page.)

Unit trusts

The heading of the prices pages is actually 'Unit Trusts and Open-Ended Investment Companies Prices'. The various units are grouped under the management company, such as Aberdeen, M&G and so on, with the addresses and telephone numbers (for trading, information, prices, etc) so one can call for application forms and information – investors do not have to go through stockbrokers to buy them but can go direct to the company. Some of these companies have regular savings plans. Along with the name, some of them have a number in figures, eg (1200) F, which means the prices were set at noon (using the 24-hour clock) and the company uses forward pricing – orders are taken from investors and the price is determined from the next valuation.

FIGURE 7.5 Unit trust prices page entry, *Daily Telegraph* – as that shows OIECS are listed only with bid prices

M & G SECURITIES LTD				
PO Box 9039, Chelmsford, CM99 2XG				
Enq: 0800 390 390. UT Deal: 0800 328 3196.				
Charibond Inc..................	–		114.7	+0.1
Charibond Acc.................	–		2386.1	+0.9
Charifund Inc..................	–	908.36	908.36	–7.25
Charifund Acc..................	–	£90.44	£90.44	–0.72
Corporate Bond..............	3.0		29.89	..
Dividend Inc.....................	4.0		41.84	–0.34
Dividend Acc....................	4.0		311.36	–2.56
Managed Growth.............	–		*53.9	–0.5
Managed.........................	–		*35.01	–0.12
N.A.A.C.I.F. Inc.................	–		52.75	–0.25
N.A.A.C.I.F. Acc................	–		3412.25	–18.0
Recovery Inc....................	4.0		83.64	–0.79
Recovery Acc...................	4.0		176.3	–1.66
Global Basics Inc............	4.0		439.67	–7.31
Global Basics Acc...........	4.0		653.84	–10.88
Extra Income Inc.............	4.0		*486.77	–3.26
Extra Income Acc............	4.0		*2992.11	–20.0
UK Growth Acc................	4.0		*2052.56	–23.67
UK Growth Inc.................	4.0		*1535.15	–17.71

Noon is the most common time for setting prices. An investor telephoning an order at 11 am would be buying at a price set an hour later, but another one calling at 1 pm would have to wait until the next day for the price.

The 52-week highs and lows are similar to those for shares, but for unit trusts the papers print a buying and selling price and a change in the mid-market price from the previous ones. Some also provide a column to show yield gross as a percentage of the offer price (at which the investor buys).

Mondays

On Mondays, with no news on the trading front (readers will presumably have got the week's closing prices from the Saturday newspaper, if not off the net), the newspapers have the chance to print different or additional material.

Market capitalization is the total value of the company on the stock market at the current share price. So if Consolidated Alaskan Coconut Plantations has issued 50 million shares and they are currently being traded at 85p, the company is valued at £42.5 million at the moment and that is how much it would cost to buy all its shares. This is of no help in deciding whether it is a good buy or not, but newspapers have always printed such figures and they do at least give some indication of its standing.

If it is in the FTSE100 then it is one of the largest companies in the country, and you can gauge the market rating by combinations of price/earnings ratio, yield and market capitalization. Do not be fooled by the size though – Polly Peck was a huge company in the FTSE 100 Index just before it imploded when the man who ran it jumped bail to flee to northern Cyprus.

There is also information like the percentage change of price during the week, the last dividend (usually shown net of tax), when it was last quoted xd (ex-dividend); † in the *Financial Times* indicates an increase in the interim dividend in the current financial year and ‡ shows a decrease; dividend cover shows the number of times that level of dividend could have been paid out of the latest profits. There is often a separate table for the most recent issues.

Indices

To get a flavour of the economic circumstances and to judge the tenor of the market as a whole, a wide range of indices specify sector movements in most of the markets in the world. In Britain the most commonly used is the FTSE100. It contains the largest hundred companies by market capitalization – their worth by the total value of their issued shares. That inevitably means the constitution of the index changes as some corporations fall from grace or get taken over, and others grow or become popular. And sure enough, the Stock Exchange does indeed continuously update the constituents of the FTSE100.

A little further down the pecking order is the next crop of large companies, the FTSE250, and those two are sometimes combined into the FTSE350. Wider still is the 650 All Share (which does not in fact include all shares). The *Financial Times* produces a full list of the FTSE indices compiled and calculated under formulae developed by actuaries. Newspapers sometimes print figures for the movement of indices for industrial sectors such as engineering and machinery, or construction and building materials – which are then aggregated to form wider industrial indices such as Basic Industries, General Industrials – and some describe the type of company, such as 'small cap' (small total market value of the shares).

Every stock market around the world has its indices to indicate market movement as a whole, but the ones reproduced in Britain are generally confined to the local equivalents of the FTSE100. Some of the better known and more commonly used ones are the Dow Jones (actually the Dow Jones Industrial Average), Nasdaq 100, NYSE Composite, and Standard & Poor's for the United States, though there are larger coverage indices as well such as the Russell 2000 and the Wilshire 5000; Toronto 300 for Canada; Nikkei 225 for Japan; Hang Seng for Hong Kong; Dax for Germany; CAC40 for France; AEX for Amsterdam; BEL20 for Brussels; IBrX for the hundred largest Brazilian companies; and Eurotop 100 for the hundred largest market capitalization companies on European exchanges. There is also the MSCI world index.

In The *Daily Telegraph* there are two tables of indices on the prices page. One is for the 12 largest foreign stock markets excepting New York and Toronto, which are in the Key Markets table on the facing page (the newspaper owner is Canadian), though Tokyo's Nikkei index appears on both pages. The other table shows the major British share indices including the FTSE100 and 250 (plus the 350, which is just those two together) and the 30, which was the FTSE100's predecessor. There is also the Techmark, which is the Stock Exchange's attempt to show backing for the newcomers and high-technology companies by separating them into a go-go index, which has turned into a bit of a go-stop-go. There is also a table of the highest volumes of trade.

Online

The internet means we are no longer dependent only on the morning paper for information, though there are electronic versions of both newspapers and some magazines available, often carrying stories that will appear in the next morning's printed version. The archives can also show what they previously said about a company or the state of the economy.

Other information about investments and companies (including from their own websites), and some comment is also available. As with all internet advice and comment however, trust only those with reliable provenance, known record and evident independence.

There are many online brokers, such as Hargreaves Lansdown (www.h-l.co.uk), some of which offer commentaries, as well as 'real time' prices (the ones being quoted at that moment on the Exchange computers), occasionally for an additional subscription. The advantage is that you can deal immediately on the information and at the price. In addition, there are news services such as www.bloomberg.com and specialist services such as www.thestreet.com.

Other online sites worth exploring are Home & Finance (www.fmlx.com) for investment tools; the publishers of the *Company Guide* and *REFS* (www.hemscott.co.uk); Moneyworld for share prices, indices, new issues, news, etc; and www.news-review.co.uk for a summary of useful news and information.

Company accounts

Much of the analysis of suitable investments for both professionals and private investors starts with the company's annual report and accounts, and most of the ratios are calculated from figures taken from the annual report. Most companies will be happy to forward a copy on request and large numbers of them are available on the internet from Company Annual Reports On-Line (CAROL). Quite often, companies put their accounts on their websites, and they can usually be found on the investor home page.

Annual reports and accounts are formidable documents apparently designed to ward off insomnia in all but the most dedicated. But you don't get owt for nowt – investing your time before investing your money reduces the chances of doing something spectacularly silly. So it is worth learning a little of the meanings behind the figures, and the conventions used to prepare them. For a true understanding of a business and how the company fares one really needs to talk to production foremen, sales staff, van drivers, internal auditors, purchasing managers and the finance director to supplement the picture from the published figures. Unhappily this is not open to investors, though it would be for stockbrokers' analysts if they bothered to avail themselves of it.

The first rule to remember is not to be taken in by the spurious accuracy of having it all set down in precise-looking numbers. Everything in the annual report is the result of approximation, estimation, interpretation or guess. Accounting standards may limit the range of flexibility but the company still has scope for a pretty fair range of subjective assessment. That is in part because the rules themselves have to apply to a wide range of types and size of business and an enormous range of circumstances. As even the Accounting Standards Board conceded many years ago, corporate accounts can be relevant or comparable, but not both. It has in the main gone for relevance (the figures are tailored more to produce a fair picture of the business) at the expense of producing readily comparable accounts, which means investors get a better picture of the business itself but must put in some extra work to try and measure one business against another.

The second rule is that the purpose of accounts is to demonstrate that the business is being run honestly and the investors' cash is not being embezzled. There is no intention to demonstrate competence, much less efficiency, though that is what investors need. In the absence of direct hints about how clever the managers are, investors need to dig into the annual report to deduce it from the available information.

It is partly to help that process that the accounting profession has for decades gone way beyond the demands of the Companies Acts in the amount of disclosure. The theory is that if all possible information is there, crooks and fools will have nowhere to hide. On the other hand, Britain is approaching the United States in the size of corporate documents and few can sift relevance from the mountain of figures. Some of it is unquestionably helpful in getting down to the details of how the numbers relate, but that usually acts as a substitute for finding just what makes a business tick.

A company's annual report and accounts may have plenty of material for the careful calculations of stockbrokers' analysts but much of it will be incomprehensible, boring or irrelevant to most investors. Nevertheless the document does contain the occasional gems that indicate where the company is going and whether it is headed for riches or the knackers' yard.

Relying on the auditors too heavily is a mistake. They are accountants, nominally appointed by shareholders but in practice by directors, who are supposed to take an outsider's dispassionate view of the figures and to see that they have some relation to reality. Their main criteria are supposed to be derived from the requirement that the accounts represent a true and fair view, but increasingly they prefer the less contentious approach of saying the figures have been compiled in line with the rules. Even when they are conscientious, independent and rigorous, auditors are governed by the same uncertainties in the figures as the company itself, and in any case they cannot possibly check everything. As they themselves keep saying, they are guard-dogs, not bloodhounds – in other words they are there to check the figures add up and the stocks really are in the warehouse but do not see their job as hunting through the business for signs of fraud or even incompetence. That is why auditors clearly say at the end of the report it was the directors who prepared the accounts and who must take responsibility for them.

Such statements are also an attempt at a pre-emptive defence against litigation. When companies go under or are found to have been subject to massive fraud, creditors sue auditors because they have large professional indemnity insurance, rather than directors who may have carefully salted money away in overseas trusts or their spouses' names and therefore seem to be people of no substance. Directors are, however, responsible both in law and in fact for running the company, and shareholders should resist pressures to reduce their liability no matter how worthy the cause appears to be.

Another thing to remember is that accounts represent the past. They will not therefore necessarily give an accurate picture of where the company is now, much less where it will be in the future, especially in fast-moving trades or changing economies. Accounts are prepared on a 'going-concern' basis, which means, among other things, that assets are valued not by how much they would fetch in a break-up but at their worth to the business.

None of this is intended to suggest that accounts are useless or misleading, merely that they need interpretation, are imprecise and represent the past. That means a little more work in trying to evaluate just what they really do suggest.

First, some conventions. Like the government, companies generally do not stick to the calendar year. Financial years start at any time, sometimes not even at the beginning of a month. There may be nothing sinister in this. Financial years start when the company was originally registered and it could be that it has just stuck with it. Some businesses reckon their sales are seasonal and set the financial year so the second half gets the benefit of the upturn.

Any number in parentheses is a negative. So, at the profit level of the accounts, £12.8 million indicates a profit but (£385,000) shows a loss. The numbers in the main pages of the accounts are mostly sums of various groups of numbers that are then shown in greater detail in the notes – there is normally a little number next to each line to show which note relates to it. It is also worth remembering that many of the numbers in the report are a bit barren on their own and have a far greater significance when related to other numbers in the accounts, set against previous years or by comparison with other businesses.

The main items in the document are the directors' report, the profit and loss account, and the balance sheet. In addition there are the extensive notes, which are supposed to amplify or explain the figures; the source and application of funds, which show where the company got its cash and how the money was used; and the auditors' report.

Chairman's and directors' report

Right at the front is a brief word from the chairman and the directors' report. These should say what the company does and sum up significant highlights of the year just completed, possibly with some comments on the performance and how the figures should be interpreted. There is often a word about prospects, which is only fair considering most reports are produced several months into the next financial year, but seldom give more than a cursory suggestion. The usual formula is something like, 'Despite the difficult financial circumstances we hope to continue developing the company and hope for further improvement in the results for the current year.' If the results turn out worse, shareholders cannot sue for misrepresentation even on that small scale and, to be fair, even three months into a year may give a misleading picture of the results for the whole 12 months. One has therefore to learn to read between the lines and see what the phrases indicate and what the report is hinting at. Some do try to be as explicit as circumstances permit, and so can offer a veiled message.

Accounting policies

Most of this is extremely boring and can safely be ignored as routine prescribed by the laws and accounting standards. Just occasionally, however, a company reckons the standard rules would produce nonsense and, rather than mislead, it intends to depart from the normal presentation. The report then should explain what standard is being breached and why. The explanation of this may not always be the most lucid prose and is not primarily aimed at the layperson, but a bit of careful attention will usually unravel it. If the auditors reckon it is a bit of flummery or specious excuse they will comment on it in their report.

Profit and loss account

Turnover

The profit and loss account starts by showing the company's trading over the previous financial year. That shows turnover, which just means sales and sometimes is actually labelled so. Drinks companies sometimes then take off excise taxes to show net sales value. One can then see how this latest year compared with the previous one. Even if it looks healthy it is probably wise to flip to the note associated with the figure and see if there are breakdowns. Some companies show the sales by product, by geographical area, by market sector and so on. This will show whether there are any peculiarities, like one product supporting the sagging rest or one geographical area turning distinctly dodgy. If there is anything like that, turn to the chairman's and directors' reports to see if there is any explanation. The answer may be something simple like an acquisition or a disposal. If there is no explanation, such distortions or odd figures should prompt questions and trigger caution.

Operating profit

Next are the operating costs of running the company including everything from stationery to wages, which are often broken down into major components such as cost of manufacturing, distribution, administration, and research and development. These can sometimes suggest questions, such as: why is administration so expensive, or why has the company been cutting back on research for several years? When the cost of sales is deducted from the total turnover figure, the result is the operating profit.

Other incomes

In larger companies you then get a variety of other incomes such as money paid to the parent company by subsidiaries, or occasionally the other way, and some exceptional items that are not the normal part of the company's trading operations. A business has to pay interest on money it has borrowed. Any sharp movement in interest out or in that is out of line with prevailing interest rates should prompt searches in the notes and statements for explanations. It could be borrowings for acquisitions or for a large redundancy programme.

Pre-tax profit

When the operating costs and other incomes have been accounted for, what is left is the pre-tax profit, which is the figure normally used in newspaper accounts of results. Taking off Corporation Tax and dividend payments leaves retained profit, which the business is planning to reinvest.

Accounting standards say exceptional items such as profit from the sale of an office building or the cost of a major reorganization and redundancy of many employees, have to be separated out.

Other items

The other items are fairly straightforward. The profit and loss table shows the amount being paid to shareholders in dividends, sometimes with preference shares separated out. Anything left after that is transferred to reserves. This does not mean it goes into the company coffers, and the term is confusing, so some companies have opted instead to call the amount 'retained profits' or, to be even more explanatory, something like 'profits retained in the business'. This is the money that builds the company. It goes into buying machinery, factories or raw materials, or financing work in progress. Some companies have starved themselves of this vital reinvestment because institutional shareholders demand a growing dividend cheque every year even if that means depriving the enterprise of cash – if the business suffers they will just ditch the shares and move on to another company.

There is nothing in the accounts that would suggest, for instance, a good start to the year but the whole business falling out of bed in its last three months with plunging sales and profits. All of that should be mentioned in the reports from chairman and directors with explanations as to why it happened and what they are doing about it.

A cliché is to talk about the bottom line, which is reckoned to come from the accounts. In fact the bottom line of the profit and loss account, after the retained profits figure, is usually the earnings per share. Dividing the share price by this figure provides the P/E ratio, or to be precise the historic P/E.

Balance sheet

While profit and loss accounts show an accumulation of transactions over the whole financial year, the balance sheet is the picture (traditionally called a 'snapshot' to emphasize how briefly relevant it is) of the financial position and assets on the last day of a company's financial year. Everything it owns or is owed on that day is shown under a range of headings. By the time shareholders see the totals, the figures are largely irrelevant because in the intervening months everything could have changed.

The figures are, as with much else in the accounts, open to a degree of flexibility. For instance, valuations of assets are fairly subjective and depend on the purpose for which the figure is being prepared. A machine tool may be vital for the company but would fetch little if the liquidator had to break up the assets. Setting a price on patents, trademarks or brand names is even dodgier and there have been years of arguments about the true valuation of such intangible assets. The physical assets and stocks are often shown at cost, but inflation will have eroded that even if other factors have not altered the valuation. Similarly, land values can move sharply with the vagaries of the economy and the property market.

What the accounts will show is the depreciation reducing the worth of assets. The notes and accounting policies usually elaborate on this, but it is normal for machinery to be written down by a fixed amount each year – straight-line depreciation. Clearly that leaves ample room for a bit of a nudge or window-dressing by adjusting valuations or bringing forward some items and delaying others, to give the total figure the company wants to project. The snapshot may therefore be wholly atypical of the state of its finances on any other day of the year. Despite that, it gives a hint of the financial health of the business, all the more so since the range of manipulations

– short of outright fraud – is limited for a number of reasons including accounting standards and the need to be reasonably consistent with the previous years.

In the list of things the company owns the first heading is fixed assets. This comprises things that have been and are likely to continue as long-term investments. So it includes things like factories and equipment, office blocks and the like. Lorries are also included under this heading, probably for want of a better place to put them. The value is normally in there at cost or what they would sell for, or some formula.

Then come investments in other companies. Then there are current assets, which covers the more mobile, changing things like stocks of raw materials and finished products in the warehouse, money owed by customers, and money in the bank.

After that comes a list of the company's debts. First there are current liabilities, or creditors expecting to be paid in under a year. This includes trade creditors (suppliers of goods and services who have not yet been paid), money borrowed short term, the money set aside for the proposed dividend, and the Corporation Tax to be paid on the profits. The total is then deducted from the current assets to show the net figure. This is sometimes called 'working capital'.

Longer-term debt includes things like a term-loan from the bank and provisions for known spending such as restructuring the business, moving the factory or the feared outcome of a legal case. Taking the short- and long-term liabilities from the assets produces the net asset figure.

Once again, there should be comparison not only with the previous year, which most companies provide, but also with the previous five years. Combining the current figure with previous years' and knowing something about the norms in that industry should provide a pretty good measure of the company's financial health.

Cash-flow statement

Cash flow, or flow of funds, or source and application of funds statements are, as the names suggest, a supplementary indication of how the money flows in from profits and investments, and goes out again for tax, dividends and the like. In addition it gives the figures for repayment of capital – redeeming a debenture, for instance – or finance in from raising further capital. There is little point in making a profit if the business just runs out of cash, and this is where the warning should show.

The final figure of the statement shows the growth or decrease in the company's funds during the year. That is a fairly good indication of how successfully it has been managed.

Auditors' report

The auditors' report is normally a pretty routine affair, saying the company has abided by the accounting standards, Companies Acts requirements and other rules; that the directors are responsible for the accounts and the auditors merely take samples and tests as required by the Auditing Practices Board; and that as far as they can tell the accounts represent a true and fair account of the state of play. Just occasionally it is a qualified report.

In essence there are two sorts of qualification, as a result of uncertainty or from disagreement with the way directors treat some item. The effect may be much the same but the message is signalled in different ways.

If the uncertainty is big enough to mention but not fundamental to the business, the auditors normally say that, subject to the specific doubts, which they will normally spell out, the accounts are all right. That may just be awaiting the outcome of a court action and hence are inherently uncertain, but it could also say the auditors could not tell if proper accounts had been kept in one part of the business.

Sometimes it is a straight disagreement about the treatment of an item. Once again, if it is a biggish number in the context of the accounts but not serious enough to undermine the survival of the organization, the auditors normally say it is all true and fair except for the specified item. The auditors may, for instance, say a debt in the balance sheet is not recoverable despite all the directors' optimism.

On a few rare occasions the split between the board and the auditors is so serious, or the auditors have stumbled on something so crucial to the company's viability, that a more serious warning is inserted into the accounts. If the doubts about record-keeping or the reliability of information generally is so great that the auditors have serious doubts about the whole thing, they will say they could not discover whether the stocks are present or the sales are as stated; they may say the books and figures were not available; some tests of the books were frustrated; or they had some deep problem about verifying what was going on and so on, and as a result they can give no opinion on whether the accounts are true and fair.

Sometimes there is just a fundamental disagreement between the directors and auditors about what things are worth or how they should be treated. If these are such major items that they are fundamental to the state of the business, the auditors normally set out the problem – say the valuation of major long-term contracts – and state that the accounts are as a result misleading. They normally add that had the accounting treatment been as they suggested, the profits would have been so many millions lower.

Such major rows are rare because the board and the auditors argue about such items at enormous length, and auditors bend over backwards to avoid such open conflicts, if only because it is almost always the prelude to a change of auditor, so the accountants will lose a source of revenue.

Another worrying comment from the auditors is that the accounts have been prepared on a going-concern basis, which is a warning that the figures would be unjustified if the business went bust. Clearly that sort of point is not going to be made about a business with a booming present and a flourishing future.

Notes

Behind all these are the notes, frequently running to dozens of pages. It is a frightening and long set of technical-looking statistics. In fact this is where the real meat is generally buried.

A series of reports on corporate governance has produced the Combined Code, which the Stock Exchange backs, that instructs companies to include mention in their annual reports of how far they complied with the requirements. In addition, some companies provide unaudited supplements giving breakdowns by product area and country of sales, sometimes by country of manufacture and other details.

This is the section where you will find how much directors earned and what sort of incentive and share-option packages they have. It will also show how many employees there are and how that total changed during the year.

Also at the back but not usually a formal part of the notes is a table showing previous years' performance, going back at least five and sometimes 10 years. That means one can check whether sales have risen faster than the rate of inflation and whether the trend has been a steady one or erratic. It also tends to show the step change when the boost to profit and turnover came not from organic growth but an acquisition.

Using the accounts

This then is the start: now these bare figures must be related to something to extract some meaning from them. For instance, the figure of the trade creditors as a percentage of turnover: the higher the percentage the longer customers are taking to pay. This means not only that the company must find expensive finance to bridge that gap, but that its cash and credit control are not very good.

Another significant figure is the relationship between borrowings and share capital. Borrowed money has to be repaid and the interest is due whether the company is making a profit or not. Equity – share capital – is never likely to be repaid and dividends are paid only when the company can afford them. If the profitability is greater than the cost of debt, the profit attributable will be geared up substantially. All the same, there are limits to how much a company may borrow, and borrowing makes a business vulnerable. The ratio between those borrowings and the equity money is called 'gearing' ('leverage' in the United States), and a company with shareholders' funds of £150 million and borrowings of £75 million would be called 50 per cent geared. It varies a bit depending on external circumstances and the industry sector, but if it went to over

60 per cent the company would be called 'highly geared'. Analysis of such ratios can be found in Chapter 6.

One aspect that is easy to study is the trends over time. All accounts provide the previous year's figures and many provide summary tables for the previous five years. These will show, for instance, whether turnover has risen faster than the rate of inflation, and whether profits have risen even faster through increased efficiency, concentration on high-margin products and so on.

Other information from companies

Interim reports

In between the annual reports companies also produce the results of trading in the first half of their financial year. These are generally pretty short documents giving a brief statement of the volume of trade and profit, plus an abbreviated balance sheet minus the copious notes. Some companies give some segmental information as well. The figures are not audited.

Prospectuses and listing particulars

Companies first coming to the stock market must provide extensive details not just about the business but the people running it. The listing rules of the Stock Exchange require all sorts of information about assets, depreciation, government grants, a brief history, auditors, bankers, financial advisers, stockbrokers, solicitors, a complete description of the business, details of management (directors have asked the government to be excused from putting in home addresses in future), staff and premises, what will be done with the money raised, expectations of the immediate future, and so on. So the prospectus is the most comprehensive information about itself that a company ever publishes.

The Alternative Investment Market has slightly less onerous demands for details, but they are still pretty extensive.

Circulars on disposals and acquisitions

Shareholders must be told of any substantial acquisition with details of the offer, why it is being made and how it is to be paid for. In most cases the shareholders will have to ratify the board's decision to purchase.

Some bids are called 'hostile', though it is the business on the receiving end of an unwelcome offer that is belligerent. In such non-agreed takeover battles the target company will send shareholders documents defending its management and trading record, and emphasizing its glowing future as well as the need for continued independence. These tend to be accompanied by extensive disclosures, accounts and forecasts, rivalling the annual report in scope. Sometimes a higher offer seems to conquer such emphatic misgivings.

Newsletters

Shareholder loyalty has grown in importance in recent years, so companies try to keep their investors happy by sending them newsletters. Even more commonly, there are magazines and newssheets distributed to employees, who sometimes also get a shortened version of the annual accounts. Careless companies sometimes tell a different story in house magazines and shareholder reports.

Other sources

Share buy-backs

A company buying back its own shares should suggest questions. Is it because the business has surplus cash and can find no way of growing the business? Is it a failure of management in finding nothing in the business in which to invest? Is it just an attempt to make its figures look better by boosting the earnings per share, and increasing its share price? Or is it a sign that the business thinks this more sensible than buying overpriced assets through a business takeover?

The shares bought back can be cancelled by the company or kept in 'treasury' for release at a later date.

Directors' dealings

Companies are obliged to tell the Stock Exchange authorities about dealings in their shares by directors. This goes out on the Stock Exchange's news system and is occasionally picked up by an increasing number of newspapers.

Directors may provide very plausible reasons for selling, but it is best all the same to be wary and check what is going on. The director may really need the money for the children's education, to pay death duties, to buy a small chateau in the Dordogne, or to fund a contentious and expensive divorce. But even then, why did that director sell those shares to find the money? Without convincing explanations, one really does wonder what the managers of a business know that other shareholders do not when they start selling the shares in substantial quantities.

Conversely, the fact that several board members seem anxious to increase their holdings does seem pretty encouraging even if they are not acting on insider information. Directors are allowed to trade in shares only when they are not in a 'closed period' of sitting on sensitive information, such as the company's latest set of results or news of a contract won.

Fashion

Fads overtake the world of investment with even greater virulence than women's clothing, and are equally evanescent. The internet bubble is an example, but at least that was related to some underlying business opportunity. It really was true that the system was changing the way people do business, but nobody knew how much or how quickly, much less who was going to win during the trading revolution. As a result there was no obvious way of valuing an internet company. Valuation was made additionally difficult by the variety of software producers, internet service providers, retailers, etc. P/E ratios became insane or irrelevant (there were no earnings yet) and everyone knew the businesses were overvalued, but there seemed no way of stopping the boom – until it stopped.

Unlike the internet fashion, which at least derived from some confused perception of what really was going on, some fashions seem based on nothing but vaporous unrealistic hope. The point here is twofold: it is not wrong to invest in a promising sector such as the internet so long as you can see real value in the business, but it is folly to get caught in the hysteria; and it is vital to separate the booms that are based on real business opportunities from the ones that are nothing but passing fads apparently created by some sort of market ramp.

Sometimes a big takeover in a sector – banking, insurance, pharmaceuticals, retailing and so on – prompts speculation that others will follow, and most of the shares in similar businesses suddenly romp ahead. Whether there is a sheep-like mentality in business, whether financial advisers then see the chance of income and urge their clients to grab a share of what is left, or whether managements really do fear being left behind, the speculation quite often becomes fact. It happened with the demutualization of building societies and insurance companies. When one of those became a public company, owners of the others could not resist the lure of short-term profits and forced a flurry of demutualizations.

When there is a general realignment in the industry of this type, the people who spot it at the start and buy into the companies likely to become takeover targets see healthy rises in the shares. Similarly, carpetbaggers getting into the building societies in time emerge with a few thousand pounds of shares that they can swiftly extract.

Another fashion is for sectors. Suddenly biotechnology is seen as the saviour of mankind with untold riches to be derived from new drugs; software companies are seen as the universal traders; the internet is thought to be a guaranteed means of selling to hundreds of millions of people at no cost at all; or a mining sector is reckoned to be certain to make a fortune from the spurt of demand for its metals. Vogues of this type seldom last more than a year, so it takes nimble minds to spot the trends, but the results can be spectacular. It is possible to increase the value of the holding by anything from five-fold to 20-fold in a matter of months. The point is to get out before the sky falls in.

Conversely, it is dangerous to climb aboard a bandwagon if it seems to have no real engine. If you do not understand what a company does or why it is valued as highly as it seems to be, avoid it.

Stockbrokers/investment advisers

If you have a stockbroker who is providing more than just a dealing service, or an investment adviser, there will be ample advice and information on tap. It may be very good advice, but intelligent investors are not wholly inert, prepared to accept everything they are told. You get better advice if you are informed enough to be able to discuss the market and your needs in an intelligent manner. The investor needs to be continuously keeping up to date and to have his or her priorities clear. This is not just a useful antidote to being baffled by pretentious jargon: it also helps establish whether one's ideas are right.

People without a regular financial adviser and those who distrust the advice they get have to hunt around for other sources. Stockbrokers' circulars are still generally available to them either directly or through the press, but usually after favoured clients have been told the conclusions and have had time to act on them. This is useful information because it gives a lot of background about a business, the calculations and feelings of a professional, and an indication of how the City may view the shares. You can then check what you feel, what the share price is doing and so on, and use the additional insight as an extra aid in decision making.

If you do not have access to a broker's advice, do not despair. Stockbrokers are as likely as anybody to be wrong. A classic case was the carmaker British Leyland. For about two years prior to its demise, investors were getting more and more nervous about the unruly unions, the shoddy workmanship, the short-sighted management and the increasing signs that the company could not make the cars the market wanted and was ill-prepared to make the profound changes needed. So its share slid steadily. Nevertheless, stockbrokers queued up throughout that inexorable tumble into insolvency to recommend the shares as a good buy.

Complaints

If something has gone wrong – inappropriate advice, the investor being badly treated, or instructions not being followed – the first and most obvious step is to take it up with the company concerned. Brokers and advisers all now have a compliance officer whose job is to ensure that the rules are followed and to take action when they have not been.

If that fails, the next step is to take the problem to the ombudsman and/or the regulatory authority. This shows the importance of ensuring from the outset that one is dealing with a properly recognized and authorized firm.

Chapter Eight
What does it take to deal in shares?

Most advisers reckon £2,000 is the smallest sensible amount for a single investment, though many recommend £3,000. It is possible to deal in smaller amounts at one time but it puts up an extra barrier to making a return: stockbrokers set a minimum price on transactions and the dealing costs can overwhelm the profit from the transaction. If you are dealing in a small company's shares that have a wide price spread (the difference between the buying and selling price) the threshold for potential profit is raised still further. And there is also a government tax on dealing.

For example, if the dealing cost is £20 for a £500 parcel, the share has to rise by more than 8 per cent just to break even, bearing in mind the likely dealing spread. That means a share standing at 220p would have to rise by over 18p before the investor saw any benefit. It can happen, but it is just stacking the odds against yourself. However, competition among stockbrokers is increasing with the numbers of sites on the internet growing daily, so the cost could start coming down and with it the minimum economic investment.

Mark Twain said there was nothing wrong with putting all your eggs in one basket, but *watch that basket*. That is unlikely to work for the stock market. Scrutinize a company with all the attention possible, analyse its figures and read all the reports available and, despite all the favourable indications, it can still decline, to general surprise. Sudden external changes can overwhelm sound businesses, and inept managers can so fail to keep track of what is happening under their noses that nobody outside notices either until profit warnings show the depth of the problems, or takeover predators or the liquidator move in.

For safety, therefore, one needs to spread the risks over a number of companies. A decent portfolio even for a relatively small investor would contain at least 10 companies. That is the eventual safe haven however, and it does not mean everyone must start with at least £20,000 going spare for it to be worth even thinking about the stock market – it just means these are the sensible requirements to reduce the much-publicized risks. Remember the main aim of investing is to get a decent return for an acceptable risk. With one share the risk is greater, but the more companies' shares you own the less chance there is of your entire stock market holding suddenly collapsing to nothing. It is possible to build a range of shares over the years; indeed most advisers reckon it is a good idea to keep a little float of available cash to take advantage of opportunities.

A really rich investor can put money into property, fine art, venture capital, currency funds, etc, and spread equity investment all round the sectors and the world. That way all risks are hedged. For most of us, offsetting one or two of the dangers is the best we can hope for. The two most obvious risks are that the money will be eroded by inflation, and that all of it will disappear through corporate incompetence.

It is a general rule that the lower the risk, the lower the return – which generates its own obvious warning that if somebody is offering mouth-watering returns or even a profit that seems markedly above comparable destinations for your cash, you may rely on it: there is a catch. The converse also holds true: the higher the risk, the higher the potential reward. Invest in a single share and if you struck it lucky the investment can multiply many times in a single year, and for some people with an appetite for danger that offsets the risk that the company could fold, taking every penny of the investor's money with it. In general this is to dramatize what really happens – in practice it is far more common for the share you own neither to burst through the roof nor crash through the cellar but to pootle along in the doldrums for months or even years, producing little movement in the price.

That £20,000 may look a formidable sum – especially if one thinks about it as the minimum safe level of holding – but set it against lifetime earnings of over £1 million for even a relatively lowly-paid household and it begins to seem a little more doable. On the other hand, if the total costs listed here and the amount needed to provide a reasonably safe income seem out of reach, there are less daunting alternatives, though still with a link to the benefits of the stock exchange, such as investment or unit trusts (see Chapter 3).

Investment clubs

An alternative to managed, pooled vehicles looked after by a professional is an investment club. This is a group of private investors who pool their cash and jointly decide how it should be invested. This has the advantage of spreading holdings over a larger number of investments than any single member could manage, without having to pay the fees of a unit or investment trust or other professional management company. You forfeit the expertise of the unit and investment trust people but have the fun of picking your own shares (or any sort of investment) and get a social occasion thrown in as a bonus. The attractions are becoming more well known: in 1997 there were about 350 clubs, but the London Stock Exchange estimates there were 5,000 by 2009.

The ideal number of members for a club is somewhere between three and 20. With more than 20 members the club will be called a corporation by the Revenue and you will have to start paying Corporation Tax.

The specialist charity ProShare publishes a handbook with some useful advice on how to go about starting a club; most experts recommend members read other guidance as well to get a broad range of expertise. It is not vital any member really knows about the intricacies of the stock market, but it is handy to have a range of knowledge among members about, say, engineering, brewing, retailing and so on.

It is vital to get the organization set up on a formal basis or there could be some very painful surprises and arguments later. There are model rules and constitutions available, which everyone has to sign. These set out, among other things, how people may join and leave, a unit valuation system and how decisions are made. A wide range of other issues need to be agreed: the level of monthly subscriptions; when and where the members meet; how decisions are made; appointing a chair, treasurer, and secretary; and deciding on bankers, stockbrokers and accountants. You have also to decide whether the club will continue to accumulate a portfolio or whether it is to have a finite life of, say, five years, after which the proceeds are shared out among the members. Some have specified that there be no recriminations if an investment goes wrong. Also, some formal mechanism has to be set up for the holdings. They can be held by one member on behalf of the rest (usually the treasurer), or by a nominee company set up for the purpose, or even by a bank. Several stockbrokers have packages for investment clubs.

You might be invited to join an existing club, in which case it is wise to check that all these decisions have already been made and are in accord with the sort of thing that feels comfortable. Also check that the monthly contribution is in line with what you can afford or would want to put in.

If this route sounds fun, there are still some basic considerations to prevent tears later. First, only get together with people you like and trust, and whose objectives and preferences are similar to your own. If you fancy taking a punt on the latest high-technology start-up or going for risky recovery stocks, it would be a mistake to join a club whose members reckon buying into Vodafone is pretty racy.

The criteria for choosing investments vary widely among the clubs but many opt for the riskier end of the market because the club participation is additional to the investments members have already made on their own behalf. So, they are generally fairly ready to go for Aim, technology stocks and the like. Some even extend beyond the stock market and invest in property, directly or indirectly. The main advice of the experts is not to invest in anything you do not understand and most professionals strongly suggest avoiding the complex and risky end of the market, like derivatives.

Second, it is not a free ride where you can relax on the coat-tails of more expert and hardworking members. Most clubs share out the work and make it clear they expect people to participate beyond just putting in the monthly money, even fining them if they turn up late for meetings.

Most clubs invest well under £100 a month – a common figure is about £20 to £40 – so this is not the prerogative of the wealthy. Conversely, it is unlikely the proceeds will allow anyone to retire at 30 or buy a Caribbean island. But you never know – the Hampshire village of Whiteparish has a club that managed a 49 per cent return on its investments (and won the prize for being the best), and even some children's clubs have managed returns pretty close to that. Several have built portfolios worth £500,000. Only a few have done so badly that members have lost their cash.

Costs

As with so many other things, it is more expensive in Britain to trade in shares than in many other industrialized countries. International comparisons have shown cheaper dealing overseas and fewer complaints about speed and information. Some US brokers also allow small investors a chance to get in on the ground floor by participating in a flotation – what they call there an 'initial public offering', or IPO.

Not that the US brokers themselves are universally regarded as kindly philanthropists. There is an old classic book about Wall Street, reprinted regularly over the past 40 years, which comments on the wealth of brokers – it is called *Where Are the Customers' Yachts?* Competition and technology may be changing all that.

For all the loud proclamations by the Stock Exchange, small individual holders are still considered a nuisance. Small investors deal in small amounts, which cost just as much to transact as large deals, and the shareholders need elaborate protection from sharks and their own folly because they might sue or generate snide stories in the newspapers, and MPs are likely to kick up a self-interested fuss. However, the market needs the small investor as a counterweight to the unimaginative short-termism of the major institutional holders. Private investors generally also provide a market for smaller companies that are not practical investments for major finance houses.

Brokers' commission

The main cost of dealing comes from the broker's commission. It varies depending on the type of broker, the amount of work being done, and the size of the deal.

Some charge as little as £5 minimum for dealing, but most brokers charge around £12 to £15 minimum per transaction, though there are brokers going as high as £20 to £25, with a commission on a sliding scale above the minimum, depending on the value of the transaction. An order of £2,500 might cost 1.5 per cent, with the rate falling to 0.75 per cent or sometimes even lower on major deals. There may also be a one-off charge of at least £10 for joining Crest, the Stock Exchange's electronic registry of share holdings.

A site on the internet called www.fool.co.uk provides a guide to charges of net and telephone brokers. It is not comprehensive and sometimes misses a new service or special offers from some of the participants. It is not unusual for a new entrant to buy a bit of market share by enticing in the passing investor through having an introductory period free of charges. Other online comparison sites suggest other options but all further information needs examination.

The spread

There is also the cost of trading. As anyone who has ever tried to sell a second-hand car knows, the price of something is very different depending on whether you are buying or selling. So it is with shares, which is fair enough because the trader needs to eat as well. To make sure the dealer does not starve, this 'spread' varies with the risk. So FTSE100 companies like Vodafone, Barclays Bank, British Airways, etc, which have huge market capitalizations, thousands of shareholders and a regular flock of deals every day, would have a relatively narrow spread of under 1 per cent, and some may drop as low as 0.03 per cent; by contrast a tiny company with few shareholders and little trade could have a spread of around 10 per cent.

This makes small companies and their shareholders unhappy because it creates a vicious circle. It is much harder to make a profit from small-company shares because the price has to rise far more to offset the wide spread. That deters all but the hardiest optimists, which therefore means fewer trades in the shares, so reinforcing the wide spread.

Advice and portfolio management

If you use a financial adviser to help pick investments, there is obviously a charge for the research and for the expertise in sifting the results to provide the advice.

Some people get a real buzz from organizing their investments. The combination of gambler's hunch, rational analysis, the prospect of profit, a chance to outsmart the highly paid professionals, and the arcane language of finance combine to produce a fascinating pursuit for some people. That is lovely because it creates the best sort of hobby – the sort that makes money.

Without that confidence, enthusiasm and time, one can still look after the investments but on a more intermittent basis. These are the people who read the City pages of the newspapers and keep up to date with the economic trends; they revalue their investments reasonably regularly and then decide what the best course might be.

As with advice, another option is to subcontract that work and get professional help, not just with building but also with managing a portfolio. Though some independent financial advisers and asset management companies will take on portfolios from £25,000 upwards, many of the companies are reluctant to look at you with less than £50,000 to play with. The fee structure means it would probably not be worth it if they did – and many managers prefer more than £100,000. This can be done through a formal scheme. That brings advice and comment from the stockbroker but still leaves the final decision on buying and selling and the amounts to be put in to the investor.

Another alternative is 'discretionary' management, which passes on the preferences and criteria (see Chapters 5 and 6 on how to sort those out) to the broker/manager, who then takes on the job of picking both the stocks and the timing. All this costs money of course – either a flat fee of, say, £1,000 a year, or a percentage of the portfolio managed, which can be 0.5 to 1 per cent depending on size. It goes without saying that you only give this sort of power over your personal finances to someone you trust, but even then keep an eye on them: some stockbrokers have been disciplined for 'churning' – continuously buying and selling to generate commission for themselves.

It is up to the individual to decide whether the advice, information and management are worth the cost. For most novices it may well be, but as they get more experienced, learn how to ferret out financial data, and get used to the way it is presented in newspapers and magazines, many decide to strike out alone. Either way, if a financial adviser is looking after strategy or portfolio management, do check from time to time whether the investment performance has been better than average, as that could easily have been achieved by investing in a tracker fund or exchange traded fund. Even if it is better, a second calculation should show that the performance was sufficiently better to more than offset the management fees.

Tax

After the market-makers, stockbrokers and advisers have taken their fees, the government takes its additional cut from our savings through a tax called stamp duty at the rate of 0.5 per cent on the value of every deal in UK equities, even though it was made using income that had already been taxed. For more on taxation, see Chapter 12.

Chapter Nine
How to trade in shares

Investors should understand that what is good for the croupier is not good for the customer. A hyperactive stock market is the pickpocket of enterprise.

Warren Buffett, Chairman, Berkshire Hathaway

The stock market is not in its fundamentals greatly different from the new Covent Garden, Smithfield or Billingsgate markets. Whether you are dealing in turnips, pork or haddock, or the shares of Marks & Spencer, it is just a matter of buyers, sellers, an agreed price, and usually a middleman. And just as the food markets do not encourage people to amble in and ask for half a pound of carrots, so the Stock Exchange is nervous about private investors poking into its electronics and therefore requires an intermediary to feed the investor's instructions into the computer.

In Britain the first recorded joint-stock company (as they were then called) was founded in 1553 to finance an expedition to the Orient via a north-east passage. Two of the ships sheltered from storms in northern Scandinavia and all the officers and crew froze to death. The third managed to reach Archangel and then went overland to Moscow – which was as near to the Orient as they got – where the Tsar, Ivan the Terrible, agreed a trading link. That seemed good enough: the link created business confidence, so others followed the technique for raising money.

With the growing number of joint-stock companies being created, a secondary business arose to trade holdings. As with so many of London's financial institutions (Lloyd's of London, the insurance market and the Baltic Exchange are other examples), it grew out of a coffee house, in this case New Jonathan's. As business grew, the traders moved into a succession of their own premises and in 1773 acquired the name of Stock Exchange.

It has not been an untroubled history. One of the most notorious disasters is the South Sea Bubble. It was not unique either in the shady background or the unhappy consequences.

There used to be 20 other exchanges around the country but they were amalgamated into the one at Threadneedle Street, next to the Bank of England. The rather grand building is now almost wholly superfluous – it does not even house the computer that looks after the trading. The market's current full official name is the International Stock Exchange of the United Kingdom, generally referred to as just the London Stock Exchange. It has two main components: first, the official list, which is the main market of major companies. This is divided up into groupings by trade. There is a section for distribution, one for banks, another for breweries, plus one called Techmark (or techMARK as the Stock Exchange calls it in an attempt at trendiness in its typography) for high-tech companies. Second, there is the Alternative Investment Market, which is for young companies which, by their nature, do not have the trading record demanded for a full listing.

How to buy and sell shares

One important difference from the world of meat and veg is that in stock markets one is at several stages removed from the real world. It is not just that the shares represent an interest in a company that may be miles away or even overseas, but increasingly there is not even a scrap of paper to show the ownership of that interest, merely a computer record somewhere. And as the trading becomes more electronic, with trading from one's desktop computer and with the payment being just another electronic instruction to transfer funds, it is increasingly becoming more of a computer game.

Using intermediaries

Just as with other wholesale markets, the small user needs a professional dealer to carry out the investment or sell orders. There is a range of competing firms offering services, and which one you use depends on the type of service needed, though the lines between them are increasingly blurred. Most of them have both telephone and online trading, though for some trades – such as overseas shares – some insist on telephone contact only.

It is always tricky finding the right professional firm, whether architect, dentist, solicitor or doctor, and that applies to investment intermediaries as well. It is not just a matter of financial competence, but also of technical efficiency. There are big, high street financial institutions such as banks and building societies with branches round the country and advertisements all over the place. There are also good local firms experienced in the needs of small investors that can produce performance equal to any of the biggest names in the country. And there are hosts of computer- and telephone-based intermediaries with varying specialisms, costs and services. The best way to pick the company is through recommendation, preferably from satisfied customers, or as a second best from write-ups in newspapers and magazines. Without seeing the people, the buildings, the organization and so on, it is hard to get a feel for how reputable or efficient the broker is, so an investor is driven far more to relying on reputation, recommendation and newspaper opinion.

Make sure that the broker or intermediary used is authorized and hence supervised by the City authorities. Not only does it provide reassurance of some quality monitoring, but provides a way to complain and seek compensation.

Warning

The rise in scams has prompted the Financial Services Authority and the police to issue warnings to investors. Emails or letters claiming to be from the FSA or the Financial Ombudsman asking for personal information or money are fakes – do not respond. Telephone the FSA on 0845 606 9966; the Ombudsman on 0845 080 1800.

FIGURE 9.1   Roles of the bodies in the new regulatory architecture

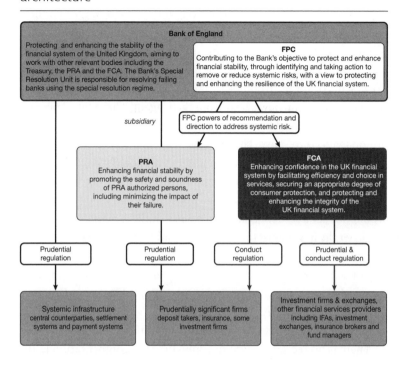

An uninvited phone call from people you do not know trying to sell shares is likely to be a scam. They are from 'boiler rooms' – bogus stockbrokers, usually based overseas (sometimes with a UK freepost forwarding address). You will almost certainly lose all the money. It is not just novice investors who are duped this way. Most of the victims are experienced investors, with 41 per cent of victims having been investing for over 11 years. The average loss is £20,000 with the biggest individual loss recorded by the City of London Police being £1.2 million. The scams net between £200 million and £500 million in the UK every year. They sometimes promise to recover money lost to the original boiler room, or to purchase those worthless shares (once an up-front fee has been paid). Some offer to buy shares you own, usually at a higher price than their market value, and ask for payment up front, as a form of security, which they say will be returned if the sale does not go through. They sometimes demand signing a form to prevent disclosure of the offer details. Some investors are encouraged to sell previously highly regarded company shares, such as banks and financial institutions and to invest in green or new technology shares, or even to take out loans to fund new investments. These fraudsters are usually well spoken and knowledgeable. They can be very persistent, phoning many times and even sending documents or forms to complete. It is an advance fee scam – they take the money and you never hear from them again. They may claim you have already entered into a contract to buy the shares and are under an obligation to pay. This is not true and such contracts are unenforceable under UK law. Fraudsters occasionally have the gall to threaten investors with police action if they refuse to go ahead with an initially agreed transaction. The police have said they "do not and would not act as a debt collection agency in these matters".

Generally it is against the law to 'cold call' trying to sell investments, so authorized firms do not contact you out of the blue offering to buy or sell shares, but there has been a dramatic increase in the fake use of names, registration numbers and addresses of people authorized by the FSA. They even copy the websites of authorized firms, making subtle changes such as using different phone numbers.

There is no recourse, right to complain or to compensation in the UK, as boiler rooms are based overseas and so not authorized by the FSA. The FSA has published lists of known scams but the names change so quickly that is little help. So if you have not invited the call, just hang up.

See also www.fsa.gov.uk/pages/consumerinformation/scamsand swindles/index.shtml and www.cityoflondon.police.uk/CityPolice/Departments/ECD/Fraud/boilerroom.htm.

If you have been contacted by an unauthorized overseas firm or suspect a boiler room scam, forward the information to the FSA or the police as they can sometimes get an overseas government to take action. The City of London Police is responsible for coordinating Operation Archway, the national intelligence reporting system for boiler room fraud: Operation Archway, City of London Police, 21 New Street, London EC2M 4TP; or PO Box 36451, London EC2M 4WN; Telephone: 020 7601 2222; E-mail: operationarchway@cityoflondon.police.uk.

Then there is the constant fear that online transactions can be eavesdropped by shady characters who might use your particulars to deal for their own profit, or hack into your or your broker's computer and tamper with data. There is always the danger of computer failures too. Computers seem to have reached about the level of development and reliability of cars in the late 1920s when drivers had to know about magnetos, drive belts and distributors to cope with the continuous breakdowns. That means, just when you need to deal, one of the machines may be having its wick trimmed or its elastic being changed. Also, online trading does not generate share certificates. The shares are still registered to the new owner, but it is all computerized and generally the broker will hold the title to them in a 'nominee' account, which is administratively tidy but could mean the investor cannot easily change allegiance to another broker.

Another danger is the seductive world of computing. Sitting at a home screen with access to all that information, it is easy to be lulled into thinking the data are comprehensive and reliable, and also into making a snap decision. It almost feels like a game using Monopoly money, so one is drawn into making investments at the click of a mouse that could wipe out the family's savings.

To join one of the growing band of online stockbrokers, one needs to get on the website and follow the instructions for registering. Many of them demand a cash account from which payments can be made, with almost all of them requiring a float of cash deposited with the brokerage. There is interest on this, but generally below what it could earn elsewhere. The signing-on procedure asks you to set a password to prevent others looking at, much less tampering with your investments, and explains the minimum level of software capability needed to get into the system.

Technical competence and infrastructure show in the speed and effectiveness of reactions to telephone calls or online contacts. Timing can be crucial in a trade and there have been complaints about the speed of reaction and indeed the ability to get anything done. In 1999 a Jersey-based investor who had his computer screen displaying share prices contacted his telephone broker and saw the value of his holdings halve while the stockbroker left him hanging on listening to a recorded message telling him all customer service operatives were busy and he would be connected as soon as one was free. He was kept on hold until somebody could be found to talk to him. So great were his irritation and frustration at watching the continuing plunge of his investments and his inability to sell that he had a fatal heart attack.

Some people, especially on the net, have had problems getting through to the broker at all and others have found the promised services permanently on the verge of arriving. Before picking a broker, therefore, a few questions are in order, such as service quality, terms and conditions, including redress in such cases.

Stockbrokers act for individual investors by executing their orders in the market, so the punter telephones the broker who holds the agreed account and gives the order to buy or sell. Quite often, during the conversation, the broker calls up the appropriate page on the computer system and tells the investor just what the price is standing at and, if that is agreeable, the deal goes ahead.

Online intermediaries usually demand investors deposit a float from which they deal but they do pay interest on the float until the money is actually invested. People are understandably reluctant to get involved in an area rife with unseen dangers. But it is changing rapidly. Customers happy to see a waiter disappear with their credit card for 20 minutes without worrying whether he was nipping up the road for a shopping spree were also prepared to read their card number out to some unknown person at the other end of the telephone for an order. These people are now increasingly buying books, CDs, holiday tickets and the like on the net and relatively few have been ripped off.

From time to time there are tales of pimply schoolboys extracting credit card numbers from online trades, but few people have lost money as a consequence and it is a lot rarer than having your car stolen or your house burgled. The danger of some hacker getting into your computer or dealing at your expense is pretty remote. Viruses are a hazard but can be avoided by having a continuously updated virus checker, which applies to anyone who goes onto the net.

There are millions of online stockbroking accounts in Europe and the number is growing. Many of these people have little loyalty to any broker or market, but will trade where it is safe, cheap and convenient.

The more adventurous, who want to buy a US share, may want to go through a US broker in the United States. It is liable to be cheaper than the British stockbrokers, and cheaper even than the European offshoots of the US brokers. A site that compares the performance of several online brokers on costs, speed of service and other benefits including helping small investors to get a subscription at the time of the first listing, is www.europeaninvestor.com.

One of the big thrills in the United States is day trading. This requires spotting the small fluctuations and getting in and out of shares within one day. For all the fashions and the hype, and despite the many books explaining how to make a fortune from the practice, it looks as if hardly any private investor has made any money on the system. Many lose heavily.

All this can be accessed and organized from anywhere, via telephones and computers, and some brokers are also introducing voice-recognition systems to provide share prices over the telephone. Whether the trading intermediary is a stockbroker or independent financial adviser, there are three basic ways the service is provided – discretionary, advisory or execution-only.

Discretionary

In effect the investor is handing over control to the adviser. It will still mean setting out the overall plan or strategy at the start, as discussed in Chapter 5: the degree of risk, the time horizon, the preference for capital growth or income, and so on. That means a prolonged preliminary discussion setting out those priorities and aims. Once the broker knows what you are trying to achieve with your money, the advice can be more sensible and helpful. After that, however, it is all up to the professional to decide what and when to buy and sell. It had therefore better be someone whose integrity, judgement and effectiveness you trust.

This approach has the advantage of using an experienced market operator with access to more information on a continuous basis than is available to a lay investor. It also has the benefit of swift reaction – the adviser/stockbroker can react immediately to a market movement and not have to wait until the investor has spotted it or gives approval. Needless to say there is a price: one has to pay for expertise.

Discretionary service demands a reasonable minimum amount of initial cash or holdings – the lowest is about £10,000 but £50,000 or £100,000 is more common, and the management fee is about 0.5 to 2 per cent of the size of the portfolio. The investor hands over the portfolio and gives the broker the right to manage as best he or she can, buying and selling as seems right. One gets a regular report of what the investments are and how much they are worth, plus notification of any dealings. Some brokers will also take into this service management of bank accounts, pensions and even insurance.

Advisory

Investors who want to retain control over the portfolio but would still like to have the professional's advice can opt for receiving suggestions. This works on the assumption that not every suggestion will lead to a trade, or it might be easier to hand the whole thing over and let the adviser get on with it. At least it allows the novice to learn the way market participants think and the sort of stimulus that prompts action, as well as getting informed opinion. It could be a type of tuition process on the road to taking over total control of one's investments.

There is obviously a fee for this service as well, though it is lower than for the complete discretionary operation.

Execution-only

Investors with the confidence that they know what they want and how to find it, with enough information and time to watch the markets, can save themselves money by going it alone. All that is needed then is to go on the website or the telephone and give instructions on what is to be done. Some of the brokers/advisers provide free services to help, such as elementary charts and portfolio valuations, as well as some highlights from stockbrokers' circulars.

Transaction-only brokers are available widely, mostly online. Information on low-cost brokers is available through tables published in many of the more serious newspapers and investment magazines.

Trading

Normally when the instruction is given to deal, the broker will transact 'at best' – buy at the lowest available price and sell at the highest. Another option is to set the broker a limit – set the maximum at which you are prepared to buy or a minimum price below which you are not prepared to sell. Usually such limits last for only 24 hours, though some brokers may be prepared to accept longer instructions of this sort.

Once the transaction is complete the broker sends a contract note detailing the deal and how much money is to change hands. It may take a little time to receive the share certificate but that is incidental since it is your presence on the share register that really determines ownership of the holding. The inconveniences can be circumvented by having the broker keep the holdings in a 'nominee' account or by having them registered in Crest, the Stock Exchange's electronic registry of share holdings.

Stock markets

Where stock markets used to have a physical presence where people met and haggled about deals, electronics has liberated them so the disseminated market is everywhere and nowhere. This is presenting the authorities with an increasingly difficult task in monitoring, and presents the investor with a growing challenge to make sure the deal is authentic, the price is right and the securities really are being transferred.

The London market operates a software called Seaq for the smallest company trades. For the majority of dealings the market uses Sets (the Stock Exchange Electronic Trading System). This is an order-matching system, so buyers and sellers post their requirements and if possible the computer matches them. Since these screens show not even the broker, much less the investor, only the two sides to the deal know the identity of the ultimate buyer and seller. There is also SETsq for the less liquid (ie less traded) securities.

Companies have been moving to Sets MM, an electronic system that involves market-makers (hence the MM) divulging their bid and offer prices. The Stock Exchange says this cuts spreads and increases the value of shares traded. The completed deal is passed to yet another computer to organize settlement. The Crest system is trying to eliminate the blizzard of paper by replacing share certificates with an electronic record in much the same way that one's hoard of gold and cash has been transformed into an item in a bank's computer memory. For the mistrustful and Luddite investors, share certificates are still available.

Many of the execution-only brokers try to simplify life by putting their investors' holdings into a 'nominee account'. That means the shares are registered to one broker account in the Stock Exchange and the companies' share registers, which make the deals quicker and cheaper.

Other markets

In addition to the traditional major stock exchanges, many of which are amalgamating across boundaries, a new breed of smaller exchanges has sprung up, some affiliated to the big ones.

Alternative Investment Market

Usually known by its initials Aim, this is actually merely a part of the stock market reserved for smaller businesses. The idea is that eventually they mature, grow and graduate onto the main market, so it is sometimes called the 'cadet branch' of the stock market. This means that younger companies with a less-solid or shorter record of profits are allowed to join. But the costs for the business of getting on to Aim are almost as high as for the full listing, so the main attraction is the lower hurdle and access to the market publicity. Another problem is that Aim shares, like smaller quoted companies on the main exchange, go in and out of fashion with institutional investors.

That provides an opportunity for the small investor. Shrewd opportunists who spotted internet stocks as having a good future when they first appeared on the Aim market made a massive amount of money, since some shares rose tenfold in a matter of days. It is no guarantee though, because the self-same shares later plummeted and some of the much-touted businesses collapsed altogether. But then smaller companies are generally more vulnerable to problems. Companies quoted on this 'junior market' can also suffer from exaggerated share price moves as they are often entrepreneurial businesses, in which the founders retain a large chunk of the shares.

Since the market was set up to provide access to young and small companies – important for advanced technology businesses – the aim was for a lighter system of regulation. But this has brought criticism, especially from rival overseas markets, that Aim companies are too lightly regulated and hence less safe.

Techmark

Worried at the criticism that the stock market was irrelevant to and provided no help for high-technology businesses, which are about to provide the future wealth of the country, and hoping to cash in on the dotcom boom, the London Stock Exchange launched an index in its market called Techmark (or techMARK as it would have it).

The principal aim was to attract companies involved with new technical ideas with the promise of rapid growth but without the trading record to be eligible for a normal quotation. As the literature points out, buying shares in this area is considerably more risky, since many of the so-called businesses are little more than a bright idea, and many of them have never seen profits.

Being in the group/index does not change how companies' securities trade since it is not a sector in itself – the companies are also grouped into the usual industry sectors, which now contain a wide range, including computers and telecoms. There are three FTSE indices covering Techmark: the Techmark All-share includes all of them; the Techmark 100 covers small and medium-sized companies; and Techmark Mediscience covers small and medium-sized pharmaceutical and healthcare companies. Their only use for investors is to help them measure their exposure to technology companies in the same way that they can use sector classifications to measure exposure to banking, engineering or retailers.

Euronext

This is the share and derivatives market created from the amalgamation of the exchanges in Amsterdam, Brussels, Lisbon and Paris plus the London International Financial Futures and Options Exchange. It therefore became the second largest in Europe, behind London.

Eurex

The German Deutsche Terminbörse and the Swiss Soffex combined to become Eurex, Europe's largest derivatives exchange.

Plus Markets

This is one of the growing number of competitors to the main London stock market. It was created in December 2005 as an evolution of Ofex, which was created in 1995 to trade shares in unlisted companies. It is designed as the first step for fledgling companies going public. They can then move on the Aim or even get a full quotation on the main market. The number of companies quoted on Plus is over 200. Around 7,500 UK and European securities can be traded on Plus. These include FTSE100 companies, European liquid shares and unlisted shares quoted on Aim. Information can be found on www.plusmarketsgroup.com

Tradepoint

A midget rival to the London Stock Exchange, Tradepoint is a completely automated electronic order book market started in 1995, which curiously enough is itself quoted on the Aim part of the main Stock Exchange. The business is 54 per cent owned by a consortium of banks including the US merchant banks Goldman Sachs and Morgan Stanley Dean Witter. It has formed an alliance with the Swiss exchange SWX to create a new exchange called Virt-X, regulated by the London authorities, in which the Swiss have a 38 per cent stake.

In addition to trading in the normal UK quoted stocks (though it has only about 1 per cent of the total trade), it has set up clearance and registry systems to allow trading in Eurotop, the 300 largest companies in Europe.

Nasdaq

Nasdaq is the acronym for the National Association of Securities Dealers Automated Quotation system. It is second only to the New York Stock Exchange (often called the Big Board) as the largest stock market in the United States and is one of the four big ones in the world. As it has kept costs of entry and administrative demands comparatively low, many young companies, especially in technology, have opted to be quoted there, including internet companies like the Amazon bookshop. Some, like Microsoft, Dell and Intel, stayed there despite their subsequent growth.

It has countered the threat of the internet-based share trading systems by forging alliances with some of them. There is a growing number of such schemes, including ones run by Bloomberg, Reuters and MarketXT. The computer-based systems can post quotes and execute trades on Nasdaq Intermarket, including in shares quoted on the New York Stock Exchange.

The operation has opened a Tokyo market, has a London office and is organizing a pan-European operation, which should make it a global exchange with a permanent and continuous trading system.

Nasdaq OMX Europe

Easdaq has used the principles and the software from Nasdaq to start a Paris-based operation but with markedly less success.

Chi-X

Chi-X started operating in March 2007, backed by Japanese investment bank Nomura. The venture claims to offer a system 10 times quicker and 10 times cheaper than existing trading systems and allows investors to deal in European stocks.

Turquoise

Like Chi-X, Turquoise is a recent rival to come on stream, providing electronic execution services to buyers and sellers of pan-European equities. It was launched in September 2008, backed by nine of the biggest investment banks, to compete directly with the main London stock market.

BATS Europe

This was founded out of the United States-based trading system BATS, marking its move into the European equities market. It went live in late 2008.

NYSE Arca Europe

This is another pan-European trading facility, which is fully integrated into the NYSE Euronext systems. It is regulated by the Dutch regulator Autoriteit Financiële Markten.

Other routes

Electronic trading exchanges may emerge. The internet is continuously providing new opportunities. Two market facilities already running are called Posit and Instinet, which are principally for institutional investors, but others are promised or at trial stages.

There is also talk of disintermediation (cutting out the middleman) by companies raising capital. Raising money by a public issue of shares is a costly business for a company, not least in the enormous fees to accountants, lawyers, stockbrokers and merchant banks. It would be attractive if all this could be bypassed by making the shares available over the net. Small investors for their part seldom get their hands on new issues because they are snapped up before they get there, or more often companies opt for the cheaper route of placing the issue with institutions. It could be dodgy for the smaller investor, however, since there will be less assurance that the professionals have crawled over the business to check its figures, managers and promises, and it is difficult to tell from the puff appearing on the screen whether a company even exists as described, much less whether its managers are competent and honest.

Chapter Ten
When to deal in shares

Never be afraid of missing the boat – it may turn out to be the Titanic.

Elliot Janeway

The early bird catches the worm, but the second mouse gets the cheese.

Stock market adage

A businessman is someone who buys at ten and is happy to get out at twelve. The other kind of man buys at ten, sees it rise to eighteen and does nothing. He is waiting for it to rise to twenty. When it drops to two he waits for it to get back to ten.

V S Naipaul, A Bend in the River

The obvious answer on 'when' questions is to buy when they are cheap and sell when they are dear. Predictably, there are problems involved, including deciding how you define cheap, finding the stock that is cheap and deciding whether it is cheap or just a poor bet. So important is this aspect that experienced investors will tell you it is more important to judge when to buy than what to buy.

One problem with the stock market is the herd instinct that drives it hither and yon on superstition, greed, fashion and uncertainty. So when the market is rising everybody piles in because they fear being left out when there are profits to be made. They are convinced that trends will continue, so no matter what has happened so far, shares are cheap because they will probably go far higher. In the reverse phase, investors private and institutional sell shares which, on most criteria, would be reckoned cheap, because they expect them to go on plunging further.

In 1710 to 1720 a series of 'bubble' companies burst onto the stock market, of which the South Sea Company (actually the full and splendidly rolling name of the enterprise was The Governor and Company of Merchants of Great Britain Trading to the South Seas and Other Parts of America and for Encouraging Fishery) was merely the most notorious. Its shares were issued at £100 and started 1720 at £128 10s 0d. By August they had reached £1,050 but finished the year back at £124 before the company collapsed. The boom was generated by mad enthusiasm over a company that took over the national debt in return for having a monopoly of trade in the Pacific. Then people realized the company was more preoccupied with ramping its shares and providing directors with a good life than with any business. That caused the bubble and the company to burst and the shockwaves sent others toppling, as banks, shops and individuals went bust as a result.

In the 1830s it was railway mania, with any company even vaguely connected with trains being relentlessly pursued by investors wanting to put yet more money into it. More recently we have had other enthusiasms. At one time being in computers was all the rage and anything to do with electronics saw its shares knock the roof off. The internet grabbed the imagination to produce eye-watering share price rises. Later the enthusiasm moved on to biotechnology when miracle drugs, 'silver bullets' and panaceas were reckoned imminent.

You can recognize a bull market reaching its peak by the unanimity of opinion that happy days are here again. Even the tabloids start talking about the stock market; there are pictures everywhere of champagne-swilling young dealers; serious economists saying this time it is different; people who would not normally know a balance sheet from a bed sheet start buying shares; and the shares themselves are on absurdly high price/earnings ratios and low yields. A sign the market is pretty well at the bottom is when share prices have been discounted for doomsday – prices have allowed for more massive slumps than it is rational to expect. In fact the share prices have anticipated so much bad news that they no longer react to it when it comes. On the other hand, the price does start to stir and rise a bit when even the slightest glimmer of good news comes along. That is the time to start hunting for good value.

The turn happens in one of two ways. There is either a sudden trigger like a huge and swift hike in the price of oil, banks suddenly realizing they have been lending money on fresh-air security, or just a lassitude when nothing seems quite right. The shares fail to respond to good news, but relapse at every sign of adverse news. That is when to stop buying, at the very least. Similarly at downturns institutions and private investors prepare for the end of capitalism as we know it. The bottom is nigh when everybody agrees the economy is sliding and will stay low for at least two years.

To be fair there is also in part a rational reason for all this: during booms people have higher disposable income both for direct investment and for pensions and insurance (with those companies then channelling part of the cash into the market), while during a recession there is unemployment, negative equity in one's home and an absence of pay rises.

When the market has been sliding for some time the careful investor will start to check whether the bottom can be in sight. You have to face the fact that you are very unlikely to buy at the absolute bottom or to sell at the very top. If you manage either, never mind both, admit it to be a pure fluke. So there are two possible timings: when it (the market, the sector, the individual share) is still heading down but one has a reasonable feeling there cannot be much further to go; and when prices have just tentatively started coming off the bottom. Get the timing wrong in a downturn and the prices will continue to tumble, and it takes a hardy soul with a gambler's instinct to go in for 'pound cost averaging' – putting the same amount in again as the price falls to get even more shares.

That sort of thinking applies to the market as a whole and also to individual shares. A very successful large company into which everyone has put their pension money for years, suddenly stumbles. It makes a few mistakes, loses some orders, miscalculates the market or whatever, and issues a profit warning. The disillusion hits the professionals so badly that they abandon the fallen star in droves.

Though small companies die in dozens and the occasional middle-rank company succumbs, it is fairly rare for a major commercial undertaking to go belly up. There have been the Leylands, Polly Pecks and the like over the years, but that is still pretty unusual, and massive collapses such as the 2008 folding of Lehman Brothers, one of Wall Street's largest banks, are thankfully rarer still. But as that shockwave-causing fall showed, they can still happen. Even if the board cannot immediately retrieve its mistakes, bring in new managers or just get back on its old track, there is a good chance somebody will be waiting to snap up the business in a takeover.

At the simplest level, much of the investor's aim can be achieved by being just counter-cyclical: see which way the herd goes and head the other way. On the other hand, it takes strong nerves to buy in a bear market when gloom and despondency suggest shares will plunge further and companies will topple over by the score. It also takes stern self-discipline to take profits in a roaring bull market knowing shares may well rise further and one is therefore forgoing some of the extra profit. There is, however, an old stock market adage for such dealing: always leave some profit for the other fellow.

Like all other contrarian views it takes caution and care. The people who specialize in this sort of investment normally wait until the first and second tumbles have worked through the market and the share price is bumping along a steady low, before starting to buy.

There are two sets of timings to consider. One concerns the market as whole, and the second is for the individual share that has already been identified (by the decisions discussed in Chapter 5). Among the factors affecting the market as a whole are:

- the general economic cycle (and that could be anything from a recovery to a slowing in anticipation of a recession);
- the level of inflation;
- interest rates, since they affect consumer demand as well as the costs of business and hence its profitability;
- tax levels and the changes;
- the relative strength of the currency, since that affects the costs of imports and the competitiveness of exporters;

- the political situation, including the proximity of elections and who is likely to win.

There are other influences as well. For instance, the London stock market reacts in sympathy with US stock markets. This provides the background for looking at and trying to extract information from recent price movements, and sets the context for examining individual companies.

At the end of the 19th century Charles H Dow, who helped start the Dow Jones Index for the Wall Street Stock Exchange as well as found the *Wall Street Journal,* detected a pattern in share price movements. He reckoned these followed a regular enough progression to be able to forecast where the price will go next.

The Dow Theory says there are great long-term patterns, called 'primary trends', which create the bull or bear markets that can dominate an economy for several years. Within that there are shorter-term fluctuations that go against the overall trend, reinforce it, or predict its turn, and these he called 'secondary reactions'. Finally, there are the daily oscillations that are called, predictably enough, 'tertiary patterns'.

The accountant Ralph Elliott worked on a grander scale. He talked of 'supercycles' lasting 150 to 200 years within which there are shorter fluctuations. There are many books on such topics, but they are probably a touch specialized for an amateur investor.

Within these grand economic cycles are price movements of the market and of individual shares, and if the trend or pattern can be spotted in time there is an opportunity for profit. This is the province of the technical analyst who relies principally on charts of market changes. At the most bloodthirsty these people assert it is not necessary to know even the name of the underlying instrument, whether it is a share, a currency or a commodity, because everything is in the price. More particularly, the price is set by market psychology and, since human behaviour is fairly constant, the pattern can be extrapolated. The trick is therefore to detect patterns in time and then act on them. That requires charts, usually of price movements.

Charts represent one of the two main ways of assessing a share. The other is fundamental analysis – the study of the company and its accounts, the markets in which it operates, and the quality of its management (see Chapter 6).

The aim of all these is to reinforce other criteria for choosing a share or a time for buying, and not to use them in isolation. That applies also to different types of chart. Checking to see how the price of a company's share moves in relation to the market as a whole is sometimes an indication to help with the decisions. Shares with a wildly fluctuating relative strength are likely to be unpredictable performers and so a more risky investment. On the other hand, if the company has for some time been sagging, with the shares consistently underperforming the market as a whole, and its relative strength starts improving, this might underline the decision to buy that was prompted by other signals. These may be better at giving added information about individual shares than about the market as a whole.

William D Gann, a mathematician and successful trader in shares and commodities, produced a variant of this, concentrating more on support and resistance levels and the speed of price change, but the explanation is well nigh incomprehensible to anyone with less mathematical expertise. Its link to Chinese horoscopes has provoked some traders into dismissing it as mumbo-jumbo.

The patterns in share prices can be explained by psychological descriptions of the way people behave, and these seem quite plausible, but not to the academics who have used mathematical analysis to produce the 'random walk' theory. This says the prices move totally unpredictably and charting the tossing of a coin would produce similar patterns. In addition, the efficient market hypothesis says information is so swiftly and uniformly disseminated that nobody can get an advantage to outperform the market. That, however, ignores the time factor, and the obvious fact that some people do very nicely indeed, thank you.

It is not quite as straightforward as a brief explanation makes it sound. Even if the random walk theory and efficient market hypothesis are dismissed as being not universally applicable, there are problems with charts. For a start they require expert interpretation of shapes that are seldom as simple and obvious as the illustrations in books. Just when does a fluctuation indicate a turn and when is it merely a temporary correction? Even with other financial knowledge to test the plausibility of an indicator, and even with extensive experience interpreting charts, the chances of making a mistake are high. That means making a fallible subjective judgement about a developing pattern, and some people are better at this than others. False signals and easily misinterpreted patterns could lead an investor into penury.

For instance, one task is to assess whether the current trend is likely to continue – if you are in a boom market, will the euphoria continue long enough to buy the shares and reap the benefits, and if it is a soggy bear market, can you predict when it is likely to turn up again? This is made all the harder by the short-term fluctuations within the longer-term movements or, as the distinguished economist Sir Alec Cairncross put it:

> A trend (to use the language of Gertrude Stein) is a trend is a trend.
> But the question is: will it bend?
> Will it alter its course,
> Through some unforeseen force,
> And come to a premature end?

The second problem is that if charts were really helpful and accessible, they would get widely adopted, other investors would rely on the developing pattern and the self-fulfilling prophecies would run away before the amateur could get involved. There would also be repeated attempts to spot the direction of development before it was complete, which would distort the shapes and cause confusion.

Professionals do not rely on charts as the trigger or guidance, but use them as an adjunct to other investment criteria. What this all boils down to is trying to get additional help on timing. That means timing not just for the individual company but for the sector and the market as a whole. That applies with equal force on when to buy or sell. A measure of how well-priced the shares are is the yield gap. That is the difference between the yield on ordinary shares and the return to maturity of gilts.

Charts

Charts are a useful adjunct for the private investor because for once there is parity with the professionals. Both have access to the same information and it is the skill in interpreting the data that makes the difference. But just as there are swarms of people with their own pet theories on how to pick the winners, so there are fanatical chartists looking for the philosopher's stone. Their greatest value is to focus the mind on the fact that in a market the correct price is what somebody is prepared to pay, so charts do provide a bit of discipline for private investors by making them concentrate on supply and demand, price and timing.

Lines

For successful predictions you have to be able to recognize the patterns that any of these lines follow; see Figure 10.1. There are the overall trends for instance – up, down or sideways – detectable by joining the peaks and troughs (or bar tips) of the fluctuating lines of prices. In a sideways market, when the price oscillates between two horizontal lines, a wise chartist waits for a 'breakout' signal when the price finally shows which way the market is now going to go.

FIGURE 10.1　Lines

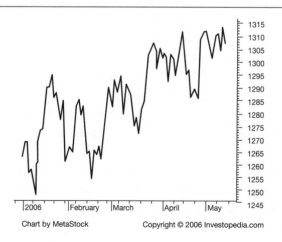

Chart by MetaStock　　　　Copyright © 2006 Investopedia.com

One answer is not to worry if the share is taking a favourable long-term path. For instance, take a company with shares that are notoriously volatile – it may look like a sideways movement but the two trend lines are a long way apart. The price bounces up and down on rumour and gloom, or profit-taking and bargain-hunting, without any obvious long-term direction. For an alert investor, that can provide a nice little earner. Just examine when and by how much it tends to oscillate and keep hopping in at the bottom and out at the top. This is safer in largish companies, which also means the gains will not be enormous, so the deals have to be large enough to offset dealing costs.

The chart patterns have graphic names to help. A 'support area' can be detected by the price dropping to but constantly rebounding from a specific price level, and there is an upward equivalent called a 'resistance level'. If the market breaks through the established resistance level, chartists reckon the price will rise substantially to a new high, and similarly in reverse for breaking through a support level.

There are also 'double tops', which as you would expect have twin peaks and indicate an imminent drop, with a 'double bottom' being the upside-down equivalent, A 'head and shoulders' is a peak flanked by two smaller peaks and indicates the reversal of an upward trend, signalling an imminent fall. Understandably, a 'reversed head and shoulders' is the same thing upside down, forecasting a rise.

'Flags' are parallelograms with a mast down at least one side when a sharp change is followed by a sideways fluctuation within a narrow range. If the flag is preceded by a rise it is usually followed by another rise, and a fall is followed by a further fall.

'Triangles' are pretty self-explanatory. The share price oscillates through a steadily smaller range. When it finally breaks out of the pattern, the direction is said to be an indicator of the way it will move for a time.

If a share has been wobbling along for a long time between two constant limits, it is said to be in a 'channel' and once again, breaking out of it is normally an indication of the new direction the price is now likely to take.

When a short moving average, such as a rolling average of 20 days crosses a longer moving average of, say, 50 days upwards, it is called a 'golden cross'. It promises a big price rise and is an even stronger indication if the two moving averages have been moving in parallel, as it indicates a reappraisal by the market. If the line crosses downwards it is called a 'dead cross' and presages a gloomy outlook.

A wealth of other patterns can be detected by the practised and imaginative chartist and they all provide some signal about the future direction of prices.

Bar charts

Bar charts have vertical lines with the top indicating the highest price traded at during the day, and the bottom representing the lowest price; see Figures 10.2 and 10.3. The closing price is shown by a short horizontal ledge on the right, and the opening price on the left. If the left opening price is lower than the close, the vertical bar is black (sometimes blue). A red bar signals the stock has gone down.

Point and figure

Point and figure charts, as shown in Figures 10.4 to 10.6, select an appropriate amount of price change that is worth recording, say 5p.

FIGURE 10.2   Bar chart

FIGURE 10.3   Bar chart

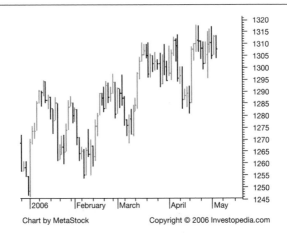

Chart by MetaStock   Copyright © 2006 Investopedia.com

If the share rises by that, the chart shows an x; another rise of that amount and another x is stacked above the first and so on until the price changes direction. Then the chartist moves to the next column and one square down from the line of crosses puts an o. If it drops another 5p there will be another o beneath that and so on. A reversal starts a new line one square up with an x. The chart ignores time, though chartists usually put the number of the month of a new stack at the top and bottom – 1 for January, 2 for February, etc – and usually start a new year with a new stack.

Candlesticks

Another type of chart that has gained interest in recent years is the 'candlestick' (previously known as the more straightforward 'bar chart'). It is much older than Dow's theories, having been used by Japanese rice traders for centuries, but works on the same assumptions: price changes move in patterns that recur and hence are predictable. Despite a small but devoted following among some professionals, including currency traders, this is widely ignored by people discussing investment.

FIGURE 10.4 Point and figure chart

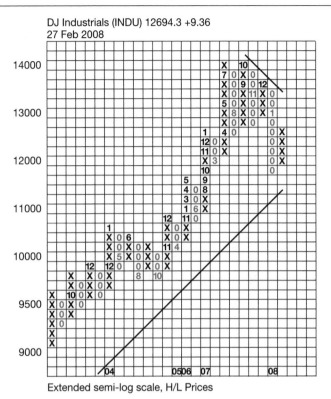

DJ Industrials (INDU) 12694.3 +9.36
27 Feb 2008

Extended semi-log scale, H/L Prices

The chart shows for each day the opening and closing prices, as well as the highest and lowest prices reached during the day (see Figures 10.7 to 10.9). Just as the Occidental charts have names for regular or significant patterns, so does this, but with an Oriental twist. There are things called 'three black crows' and 'three advancing soldiers', 'shooting stars', 'morning stars' and 'evening stars', 'hanging man', 'hammers', and so on. These charts show how trading went. So, for instance, if there is a lot of wick above the candle there must have been a rally during the day that failed to hold and will have discouraged traders. Conversely a length of wick dangling out of the bottom (called the 'hammer') shows that an abundance of sellers threatened to push the market down but there were more than enough buyers to offset them, so

FIGURE 10.5   Point and figure chart

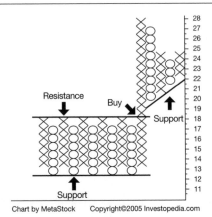

Chart by MetaStock   Copyright©2005 Investopedia.com

FIGURE 10.6   Point and figure chart

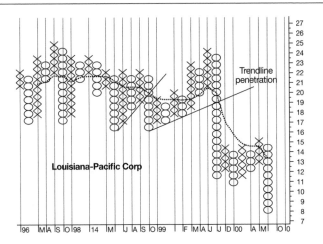

FIGURE 10.7 Candlestick chart

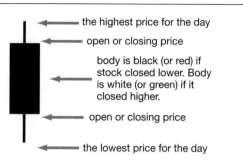

- the highest price for the day
- open or closing price
- body is black (or red) if stock closed lower. Body is white (or green) if it closed higher.
- open or closing price
- the lowest price for the day

FIGURE 10.8 Candlestick chart

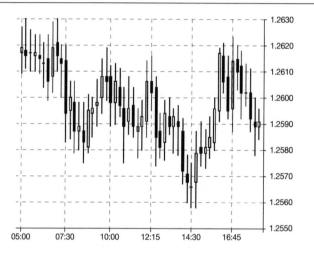

the market bounced off the bottom, which gives promise of further rises.

The wick of each candle runs from the low to the high that was reached. The wider body of the candle is between the opening and closing prices – if the closing price is lower than the opening the candle is black; if higher it is white (the original Japanese version used red for these).

FIGURE 10.9   Candlestick chart

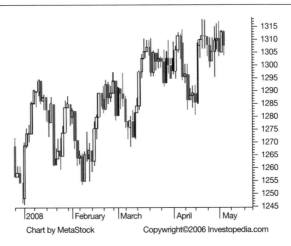

Chart by MetaStock   Copywright©2006 Investopedia.com

Technical tools

None of these charts need be used on its own. A wealth of additional information on the chart will add a level of perspective or even explanation. For instance, adding the movement of an index – whether the FTSE100, the All Share or the sector of that company – can show whether it is moving with the market. If it is not, that may prompt further research. It is also possible to see the rate of change of a price over the selected time span.

Transforming the chart line to a moving average can smooth out the daily fluctuations. Making it a weighted average gives greater weight to more recent price movements, and making it an exponential weighting adds greater sophistication. That sort of tool helps spot a trend or a change in one.

If you can find a website that also provides annotations to the charts, that would give yet another insight into what is happening and why. The most usual type of notes include dealings in the company's shares by its own directors, and newspaper or stockbroker comments on the company.

The relative strength index measures the level of a share price relative to itself and its recent history. It is calculated as the average of prices for days when the price rose, divided by the average of the prices for days when the price fell. The index ranges between 0 and 100.

Momentum

Recent price changes show the sentiment of the market, so the assumption – justified by some research – is that whatever caused them to move in one direction will continue to do so for at least a little longer. It is not invariably a sound investment policy, not just because the market is notoriously fickle, but because it requires continuously active trading at a level where any profits may be undermined by costs and tax.

For those interested in the suggestion, a stochastic oscillator can be used that shows the location of the latest closing price relative to the high/low price range over a set number of periods. It is made up of two lines that oscillate between a vertical scale of 0 to 100: one is the main line and the other is its moving average. Fast stochastic is the average of the last three values, and slow stochastic has a specified period.

Sentiment indicators

Technical analysis is not just about charts. There are hosts of other indicators providing additional or alternative pointers to market movements and hence tips on when to trade. Some of them work on indications of general sentiment in the market. One of the difficulties with any of these guides, of course, is that as soon as they become generally known they fail to provide reliable signals.

An example is the 'small-lot indicator' (small trades in shares) as a useful counter-indicator in the United States. This works on the assumption that small investors are almost invariably wrong. They buy at the top and sell at the bottom, so they provide a good counter-indicator. This has been gradually extended as it became clear it was not just the amateurs who got carried away by the prevailing or fashionable economic view: it became slightly transformed to the feeling that a universally bearish attitude in the country as a whole is a sign of an upturn and rampant bullishness is a sign to sell. Some companies even tabulate the number of investment advisers that are bullish or bearish as a sign to go the other way when unanimity seems imminent. In other words, when the small buyers start piling in it is time to sell, and vice versa. Word got around and so many people started acting on the theory that it became a self-defeating prophecy and confusion seems to have buried it.

The flow of funds indicators show demand for securities and where people are heading to put their cash. Sometimes the intensity of feeling about a company can be gauged by the volume of shares traded, especially if a chart can show whether the total is up, down or unchanged. The combination of price and volume movements gives a pretty good indication of overall attitudes:

- if prices and the amounts of shares traded are both rising it is an indication that the market for the share is set to rise;

- a rising price but a declining volume of shares traded is a worrying trend indicating the price rise is running out of steam, and as the upward movement slows to a halt the direction is likely to reverse and the price will soon start to fall;

- a falling price coupled with rising volume shows investors heading for the exit in growing numbers, which can only reinforce and accelerate the falling price;

- the price and volume of shares traded both falling shows investors beginning to have second thoughts about selling and the downward pressure is therefore easing; soon it will bottom out and start upwards.

Other indicators

There are many other systems attempting to predict market movements. Like any other activity in areas dominated by luck and the unpredictable, like fishing and acting for instance, there is quite lot of superstition involved. People are ready to grasp at any apparent correlation, no matter how dubious.

So there is one theory that sunny weather produces optimism in people generally that is reflected in prices, and another view has it that the market index moves up and down with skirt hemlines. Another old adage was 'sell in May and go away until St Leger's Day' on the assumption that everybody went away for the summer and returned for the popular horse race that marked the end of the summer lull – hence in the absence of trade, activity was listless and random. In fact any investigation shows the saying to have been unjustified when coined and becoming less reliable since.

Finally, be wary of buying on a tip or rumour. It is most unlikely you will be the first to hear it, even if it is true, and there is a very good chance it is unjustified gossip or a 'ramp' – somebody starting a story to shove up the price of shares he or she wants to sell. On the other hand, if it really is true and the information comes from someone on the inside, acting on it could land you in jail for insider trading.

One view holds that share selection is for the long term, so there is little point in reacting to every whim of stock market fashion. You bought for the long term, so hold on to the shares – an apparently sensible approach that can provide a useful overall guide but ignores the realities of life. For instance, the assumption that dictated the original decision may no longer apply – the company, the economy or the portfolio may have changed. So it is worth reviewing the decision from time to time.

Some of the guides to investment will say fatuous things like 'sell your worst shares early'. But if it were easy to tell which the worst shares were, one would not be reading a book – just because a share has dropped and another risen does not mean they will continue in the same direction, as lots of price charts will clearly show. Some old market hands are always against buying a plunging share in the hope of recovery – 'the market is trying to tell you something' they say. But if, for instance, a share goes from 23p to £12.40 in the space of 18 months and then drops back to 60p in the next six months, when did the market get it right?

So there are no obvious answers. Anybody claiming to have a simple explanation is a fool or a liar. If it were that easy everybody would have done it long ago.

There are sophisticated mathematical modelling theories about what you should do. They are interesting, some have been programmed into computers, but none of them can be justified on any logical basis. One suggests selling shares after they have fallen 8 per cent; another says sell when they have dropped 7 per cent below the top price reached.

Selling

It is never wrong to take a profit is one of the ancient rules of stock market investment. Yes, the share price may go on zooming up still further, but your profit is safe. One alternative when winning is to hedge your bets by selling part of the holding to recover the original investment plus a bit of profit, and let the rest ride just in case there is further growth left. Another of the hallowed sayings of the market comes to much the same thing: 'Leave some profit for the other chap.' This is deeply reassuring stuff, and it eases the irritation of selling when the share continues to rise – but just consider the odds against being able to buy at the bottom and sell at the top.

By some curious chance most of the advice from professionals is about how to secure your profit. The assumption is that nobody ever buys a dud. There is less helpful advice about when to join the other sleek rats heading for the shore.

In falling markets private shareholders fall into two opposing camps. There is the one Naipaul described, who hangs on to the most obvious rubbish in the hope it will eventually recover. Then there is the sort who panic at any serious drop and bail out in the expectation that once the price is heading downwards, the law of gravity will continue to operate. Both are probably wrong.

The point about private investment is that it is generally for the longish term, so the buyer should have done some pretty careful research on the business before buying its shares. The corollary is that if it continues to meet those criteria (good management, reasonable margins, innovation, good financial control, etc), then it may well be a good idea to hang on and just go on collecting dividends. On the other hand, that also means the investor must continue with the work, to see if the company is still up to snuff and therefore worth backing. If not, sell.

So much for cashing in profits or preventing further haemorrhage for a failure; that assumes the market as a whole is still healthy. The problem is spotting when the market is sick and likely to get worse, and knowing whether it is a blip or the market on the turn.

For instance, there is the time when a roaring bull market suddenly falters. This could be the result of some external trigger like a trade war or an apparently unconnected event – why the hurricane that roared across southern England in October 1987 should have triggered a plunge in prices still leaves market analysts baffled. Another cause can be a general loss of impetus. In some curious and indefinable way the enthusiasm that had buoyed up everybody and had seemed ready to continue for ever suddenly drains away. Nothing seems really satisfying. Even good news fails to lift prices, though unhappy news knocks them back. These are signals of a market on the turn and indicate that it is time to start selling before the rout starts.

Once the bear market is truly under way, selling on the way down is trickier. Professional investors are ruthless about getting out if the signs look bad, and many institutions now have computer programs that automatically start selling when a certain percentage decline has been noted. This is one of the reasons the New York stock exchanges can sometimes register accelerating falls in a share or even the market as a whole, as computers are automatically triggered to save what can be salvaged. Private shareholders, however, are always slow to sell. It is reckoned to be a mixture of ignorance (they have not been following the share's performance), sentimental attachment to a carefully chosen share, and a sort of inertia that suggests hanging on for just another day or so in case it bounces back.

The judgement is between cutting your losses and not missing out on a recovery. There are some warning signals that may suggest a discreet exit; for instance, there could be conflicting indicators and rumours about the company whose shares you hold. Another good test is to ask yourself whether the shares have become so low and the indications of good profits so convincing that the shares seem an irresistible bargain – if not, it is probably a good idea to sell. Even if you are convinced the market has got it wrong and the business will bounce back, it can be shrewd to sell. Then, if the price continues to fall and the indications are coming through that the company has turned the corner, you can always get back in.

Chapter Eleven
Consequences of being a shareholder

Shareholders are the true owners of the company, so they have lots of rights. For a start, in theory they appoint both the board of directors and the auditors. In practice the directors do both and shareholders have all too often supinely agreed to everything done in their name. Even great institutional holders who know the law and accounting principles and are sophisticated investors have been lax in exerting their power and have generally more often sold the shares than spoken up or done anything for the business. This has been changing: some institutions are using their influence and it is becoming less easy for the board to dismiss awkward questions at the annual meeting, but still too many private individuals consider any questioning of the board as an unseemly delay of their free drinks.

As owners, shareholders are entitled to be given a wide range of information, and to participate in the company's success.

Information

The information the owners must have includes regular financial facts. Every year the company must produce an account of its finances (the phrasing in law is a little more complicated but that is what the rules amount to) and this must be sent to all registered shareholders. (See Chapter 7 for what the useful information is in those annual reports and accounts and how to extract it.) Shareholders must also have notice of important events affecting the business. That includes details of major acquisitions and disposals, demergers and reorganizations.

Annual general meeting

The annual general meeting is a legal obligation and shareholders must be notified in advance. There is, however, no legal insistence that the meeting is held in a convenient spot, so if the directors are feeling bloody-minded they could hold it in the upstairs room of a pub on Stornoway. Curious times and inconvenient places for meetings, plus company announcements on Christmas Eve, are good signs to shareholders that all is not well with the business.

At the meeting they are called on to approve the accounts by voting, can ask questions and have a vote on a number of other resolutions including the reappointment of auditors and directors. Most shareholders neglect this privilege, either throwing away the voting card altogether or just sending back the enclosed proxy form giving the chairman carte blanche to vote on their behalf.

Extraordinary general meeting

Shareholders representing at least 10 per cent of the equity may demand the convening of an extraordinary general meeting.

Consultation

There is a legal obligation to consult shareholders on matters that affect the company's future. They have the right to vote on major decisions, including actions that may dilute their holdings such as rights issues and employee share options schemes. If they can muster 5 per cent of the company's equity or 100 shareholders to back them, they can even introduce their own resolutions at the meeting.

Dividends

Shareholders are entitled to take part in the company's success and profits. Normally shareholders participate in the company's profits by way of dividends, which are usually paid twice a year, but this is not a legal right since a company may decide to reinvest its profits in the business for faster growth. In practice few have the courage to refrain from paying altogether. The cheque, or notification of payment into an account, shows the size of holding and rate of dividend. Preference shares are normally entitled to a dividend, and if the company cannot for a time afford to pay, that entitlement is normally only deferred and has to be paid later when the money is available.

Scrip issues

This looks like a burst of spontaneous generosity by companies that give investors some extra shares for nothing. Sometimes they are in place of cash dividends and sometimes as a supplement to them. In fact it is a simple bookkeeping exercise that should have no effect on the share price or the value of the company – some of the retained earnings are capitalized and shifted from one line in the books to another. That is also the reason they are called 'capitalization issues'. Sometimes issuing scrip is called a 'bonus issue' and surprisingly enough, contrary to logic, the share price sometimes rises at the time. Shareholders may then find it hard to calculate the cost of the holding for capital gains tax when they sell.

Rights issues

Companies wanting to raise additional capital sometimes turn to existing shareholders first. There are several reasons for this. The first is obvious: shareholders by definition must like the company, so if it says it can see opportunities for useful investment to allow it to grow but needs additional cash, they are more likely to take a friendly view. Second, it is only fair to allow existing holders to take action against having their holdings diluted by the issue of further shares. Third, the institutions that own most of the shares on issue in Britain are especially insistent on being given the chance to maintain the percentage of the company they have decided was right for that portfolio – this is called their 'pre-emption right'.

It is a long and expensive business for a company since it must print extensive literature and post it to all holders, and the merchant banks and accountants cost a fortune in fees. A placing – ringing round funds known to be interested and asking if they would like to buy extra shares – works out a lot cheaper and can be very quick.

The opportunity to buy the new shares is allocated as a ratio of existing shares owned. It is something like the right to buy three new shares for every 11 already held, or some such formula depending on how much the company is trying to raise and how deep a discount it is offering. The issue will dilute the value of the existing shares because profits and dividends will be distributed over a larger number of shares.

Rights issues are normally offered at a discount to the prevailing share price to give people the illusion that they are getting a bargain. So if the shares stand at 200p, the company might offer one new share for every four already held at a price of 150p. So for every four shares, worth £8, they can buy another for £1.50. If investors do buy they have a holding worth £9.50 (assuming the price does not move) and the four continuing shares would be worth £7.60 (four-fifths of £9.50), but on that calculation the right would be worth 40p, so they would be back to the original £8 holding. One complication is that the money received for the rights may be taxable, and another is that the market price will react to the announcement.

Shareholders faced with a rights issue can take it up in full and pay for the new issue of shares. They can sell the nil-paid rights, which have a value on the stock market. Or they can compromise by selling enough nil-paid rights to maintain the value of the portfolio by using the proceeds to buy new shares. The nil-paid price is the difference between the discounted rights issue share price and the ex-rights price.

Nominee accounts

Many people hold their shares in nominee accounts – for SIPPs and ISAs they have to. These are held in a number of places and are a convenience to prevent shuffling of papers or to speed up the processes of buying and selling. For instance, the dealing stockbroker may hold an account for an investor, who does not therefore have to wait for share certificates to arrive before being able to sell them, and does not have to store and find the necessary papers. Some brokers offer the service free as a way of reducing their own administration; some charge a flat fee or one based on the value of the shares; yet others charge per transaction; and some large companies have instituted their own systems.

Regulated markets

In addition to their rights in relation to the company of which they own a piece, investors have a right not to be ripped off by the financial community. This is the part that is mainly watched over by the regulatory authority. It regulates British brokers and dealers, whether they are in a City office or dealing via the internet, but nobody regulates the internet. Inevitably, the net has been a happy playground for some shady operators, ranging from various types of fraudsters to people operating pyramid schemes. Some have set up bogus websites to look like the pages operated by real investment companies, in the hope of getting unsuspecting people to part with their money. In addition, the net is awash with rumours, many of them carefully placed to drive the price up or down so the instigator can sell or buy as needs be and make a killing. The authorities in the more responsible countries pursue these people, but the net is too vast to be watched.

The London Stock Exchange also regulates its own market. The Exchange's computer has a sophisticated program trying to spot unusual patterns, and if there are untoward movements in advance of an official announcement (eg a sharp rise just before a bid is disclosed), the Exchange authorities investigate. Despite some apparently suspicious circumstances, however, they hardly ever find anything untoward. Prosecutions for insider trading are rare, and convictions even rarer.

Relying on somebody else to pick up the pieces and fight the battles for feckless or foolish investing is a mistake. A little elementary care can prevent a lot of mistakes and save much effort trying to assert one's rights later. For instance, you should use only authorized businesses to act on your behalf, and that is easy to check on the register of the regulatory authority. Before starting any transactions, check the costs and fees. The first rule is, if there is anything you do not understand – go on asking for an explanation until it is crystal clear. It is much better to seem foolish by asking questions than to be foolish by not having the answers.

Codes of conduct

The apathy of most shareholders has allowed company boards so much latitude that they seemed beyond reasonable control. To fill this vacuum the City has produced a series of codes of conduct to guide directors on best practice. The latest of those, the Hampel Report (following the Cadbury and Greenbury Reports), which is backed by the Stock Exchange, suggested for instance, that:

- the task of chairing the board and the work of chief executive should be separate;
- directors should stand for re-election every three years;
- board members should not have a service contract of more than two years;
- a third of the board should be non-executives who should be independent of the company;
- shareholders should be told at least 20 days in advance of an annual general meeting;
- when raising new capital the company should give existing investors first refusal;

- any questions not answered at the annual general meeting should get written answers soon afterwards.

Takeovers

Usually, you say thank you very much. Bids for companies are almost invariably well above the price of the shares just before the bid, so shareholders benefit. On the other hand, what may well have tempted a predator is precisely that the price was standing way below any rational basis of valuation, for instance the net asset value, so it would be worth buying a business just to sell off its assets at a profit. In that case it is worth resisting, if only to get a better price.

Sometimes the offer is resisted fiercely by the target company, and the scheme for some inverted reason is then called a 'hostile takeover'. The defence usually says the bid is unwelcome and opportunistic as it undervalues the company's prospects, and the company could perform far better on its own, given the chance. The private shareholder cannot tell whether this opposition is motivated by a desire for independence, a fear of directors' losing their jobs, an attempt to get the bidder to increase the price, or a genuine feeling that shareholders would do better with the existing regime. It is, however, worth remembering that the directors' legal duty is to act in the best interests of shareholders.

The decision is made even more complicated if the offer is wholly or in part in the form of the bidder's shares. The choice is then cluttered with other considerations such as whether one wants those shares, whether the valuation of the buyer's equity is fair or realistic, and whether selling might crystallize an unwelcome capital gains tax liability.

The takeover process is monitored by the City Takeover Panel, which has no power, legal or otherwise, but manages to have its way because all the City people support it. So anybody who tries to flout its rulings would be ostracized, and once frozen out of the financial community doing business would be impossible. Being non-statutory also gives the panel the signal advantage of being able to act quickly. Moreover, it can tell participants it does not like the way they are acting – it has been known to reprimand people not for failing to follow the letter of the City Code but for neglecting its spirit. In addition it can take instant action to change the Code when a loophole has been discovered.

The panel is charging savers to supervise companies. A levy of £1 is being collected for it by stockbrokers on dealings worth more than £10,000.

It can be almost as good to own shares in a company that is in the same sector as a highly publicized acquisition. As soon as one estate agent, retailer, computer assembler, brewer or whatever has been bought, the market usually assumes a ripple of parallel acquisition activity will overtake its competitors. Their shares jump as a result. Since the flurry of copycat activity rarely materializes, especially once the targets have become expensive, it may then be a good time to sell.

Insolvency

Investing in shares is risky. There is no way of getting away from this. One of the reasons the stock market produces a higher average return than, say, putting the money into a building society or a bank savings account, is to offset this danger by compensating investors. But note the word 'average'. Some shares are more risky than others and, short of buying into hundreds of companies, the investor will be involved in shares that are a mixture: some are a success – if lucky, some of those spectacularly so; some are pretty ho-hum performers; and some, rarely, are complete collapses.

Occasionally collapses are signalled well ahead. The shares show a steep and pretty continuous slide, and the statements from the company mix profit warnings with promises of restructuring, refinancing, searching for alliances, appointing new executives and new policies on the way. This usually ends in a suspension of dealings in the shares, a move that is commonly said to be to help shareholders. Pure bunkum: it is a complete disaster for shareholders who cannot therefore sell shares at any price to rescue even a tiny portion of their investment money. The people it helps are the stock market traders who are fearful of dealing without adequate information and cannot face being swamped by people stampeding out of the company.

Companies seldom return from that sort of suspension. There are other reasons for suspension, such as during the final stages of a major acquisition, but those really are benign and are to prevent total market chaos when there is not enough known about the deal details to set a fair price. But being suspended because the company has run out of money offers few roads back.

By the time the shares are suspended they are seldom worth more than a few pence in any case. But not all collapses are so well signposted. Are there any more covert signs of impending doom that canny shareholders may be able to spot? Many people have tried drawing up signs, including Britain's top liquidator in the 1960s, Bill Mackie. The specifics of his warning signals, including flamboyant headquarters and profligate top management, may now seem dated, but the underlying principles are still sound. We may no longer have flagpoles and tanks of tropical fish but there are plenty of other loud signals that the organization thinks appearance more important than efficiency.

Investors should be monitoring the business and how it is managed. Profit margins are a good sign, so one should check whether they are as high as they were and at least as great as those at other similar companies, and whether the business is generating sufficient cash for its needs and ambitions. When external money is being raised through loans, rights issues and the like, it should be for expansion rather than baling out the current problems. Accounts being late or fudged, lack of information on auditors' qualifications, suggestions of window-dressing in the accounts and extremely sophisticated financial dealings are causes for concern. With small businesses, most of that does not apply and you have little recourse but to judge by the managers. The point about small businesses is that the profit can be spectacular but the collapses sudden.

When a company's share dealings are suspended, that is commonly a sign that the company's managers, bankers and set of insolvency accountants are going into confab. One route is for the company to try for a voluntary arrangement under which its creditors hold off knocking bits off the corporate structure to sell as a way of recovering their money and allow it to try trading out of its problems. Courts can appoint an administrator who also continues to trade and holds off creditors.

Another route is taken by secured creditors, normally the banks, which have run out of patience with the company's excuses and are worried their loans could soon become irrecoverable. They appoint a receiver with the sole task of keeping the business going just long enough to recover the banks' money. Tax authorities have also been pretty active in this route to make sure their money is paid. Occasionally the directors ask for the appointment because they can see a default on debts looming or because they are in danger of 'overtrading', which is the criminal offence of continuing in business once the company is insolvent. A specialist accountant is then appointed and moves in to run the business briefly to extract some money or sell assets for paying the debt. In theory the administrator then moves out and the company reverts to business as usual. That seldom happens in practice because the receiver's task entails selling off the assets against which the money was lent, or trading long enough to generate the cash to pay off the loan. That usually does not leave much, and the company is often passed to a liquidator.

As that name implies, the liquidator's job is to turn anything saleable into something more liquid like cash. Fire sales like that seldom produce anything like the book value of assets.

In all of these procedures there is a hierarchy of creditors, and the holder of ordinary shares stands at the back of the queue. The government takes its taxes off the top, and is followed by secured lenders with a claim on the property and employees, and the banks with other guarantees. Then there are bond holders and owners of preference shares. Once all these people have had their take there is seldom anything left for the holders of ordinary shares.

The one comforting thought is that relatively few quoted companies do actually go bust. And if your investment happens to be one of them, try and look for the silver lining: you can cash in some really profitable investments and set off the capital gains against the losses on the crashed company.

Chapter Twelve
Tax

It is galling that the government takes another slice on dividends and capital gains after it has already charged additional tax on investing taxed income. But reconcile yourself with the thought that at least you have profits to be taxed.

Tax is always complicated, and huge manuals have been written on how to cope or get the best deal possible to frustrate the efforts of HM Revenue & Customs (HMRC). This chapter represents the merest skimming of the surface and is generalized as these things change continually.

Governments have tried to steer us towards some investment vehicles by tax incentives because they think they would be good for us or for the country. It would be foolish not to take advantage of any extra benefits provided by the tax office, but it would be just as silly to invest purely for the tax break. This is especially so as the management fees for some schemes need careful scrutiny to test whether the deal is still worth it after the professionals have had their share of the cream. So weigh the alternatives and go for the one that is best, judged by your personal criteria, and only go for the savings in tax if the investment would have made sense without them.

Governments are rather good at taking money off us. There is not only tax on getting into shares – called 'stamp duty' – but also on the benefits from most kinds of investment, both on the income and the capital appreciation. Dividends, including scrip issues (see Chapter 11) and bonus shares, count as income and therefore are subject to Income Tax. Most companies pay dividends net of tax.

HMRC publishes some useful booklets on tax, including one on capital gains tax (CGT), available from all tax offices.

Dividends

Dividends on shares are almost invariably paid net of tax and the voucher that comes with the payment notification contains details of a tax credit. People who do not normally pay Income Tax cannot reclaim the tax already paid on the dividend. Those who pay tax at the basic rate need pay no further tax on the income. But people paying tax at the higher rate have to pay at 32.5 per cent of the gross, though the credit detailed in the slip is set off against this. This means that the higher-rate taxpayer will, in effect, pay top rate of tax on the gross dividend paid by the company. This complicated way of handling things means that about a quarter of the net dividend is due in tax for higher-rate payers.

So, for instance, someone owning 400 shares in Quilp & Heep Intercontinental, which pays a 15p dividend, would get a cheque for £60. Since the tax credit is 10 per cent, this represents 90 per cent of the gross dividend, which would have therefore been £66.66 (60/90 × 100). As a result, the tax credit notified with the cheque would be £6.66. Payers on the standard rate of tax are then all square, but payers at the higher rate, obliged to pay 32.5 per cent of the gross, must now calculate 66.66 × 32.5/100, which works out to £21.66. Setting off the £6.66 already paid leaves a liability of £15 to be sent to HMRC.

Scrip issues of shares in lieu of dividend (see Chapter 11) are treated in a pretty similar fashion. There is no additional tax due for people on the standard rate, and those paying the higher rate are assumed to have had a 10 per cent tax credit.

If the company buys back shares, the money received is treated as a dividend – covered by Income Tax, not CGT.

Capital profits

A profit on the sale of shares is liable to tax for profits above the basic tax-free allowance. This is a pretty handsome chunk as far as most small investors are concerned. CGT is a problem only for people dealing in largish amounts or who have really struck it lucky with one of their stocks. In other words, if the profit is so great that CGT is due, you have done so well that a bit for the exchequer seems less painful. Windfall shares received from demutualized building societies or insurance companies are counted as having cost nothing and anything made from their sale is counted as a capital gain – unless they have been put into a tax-sheltered scheme such as a SIPP or ISA.

There is a tapered tax relief, however, so holding shares for a long time will reduce the tax liability. If the shares were bought before April 1998 the price rise can be adjusted for inflation before tax is payable. Dealing costs in buying and selling are allowable against the total gain, and there is an allowance for part-paid shares. Gifts between spouses are tax-free, so the portfolio can be adjusted to benefit from the maximum allowance.

Unquoted shares are a problem since there is no publicly available unequivocal price for dealing. For these deals you will just have to haggle with the local HMRC office.

As is only fair, losses made from selling shares in the same tax year can be set off against the profit. And if any of the companies actually go bust, the shares are reckoned to have been sold at that date for nothing and the capital loss from the purchase price can also be set off against gains.

All this may help with decisions between alternative courses of buying and selling, though once again being guided purely by tax differences is usually a mistake. A good accountant can advise on such things at a relatively low cost.

Employee share schemes

Receiving shares from an employer counts as pay and so is subject to Income Tax. If the employees (and that includes directors) buy the shares at a discount to the market price, the discount portion is the part on which tax is paid.

Under approved profit-sharing schemes the company can allocate tax-free shares to workers, though as you would expect, there is a raft of rules about the details. Share option schemes that meet all the chancellor's requirements have few advantages.

Tax incentives to risk

The government wants new ideas to be financed, high-technology to get started, and innovations to be given a chance. Investment institutions such as venture capitalists will not touch them, so the tax incentives are directed at private investors. These are risky ventures and though rewards can be high for a success, the chance of failure is also pretty high. Even with the tax come-ons this is an area for people with a steady base of safe investment who also have a few hundred thousand to gamble with.

Venture capital trusts

These are really just a collective version of the Enterprise Investment Scheme it replaced. The tax breaks are similar but the investment is into a quoted financial vehicle, which in turn puts the cash into a range of entrepreneurial businesses, so the risk is reduced, as with investment and unit trusts, by spreading the money over a number of ventures.

ISAs

Individual savings accounts are part of the governments' aim to persuade us to save more of our income by providing tax incentives. Under the latest rules, you can invest £10,680 per tax year, of which £5,340 may be in cash and the rest in shares, or all can be in investments (including investment and unit trusts, OIECs, Exchange Traded Funds, or bonds). From 6 April 2011 those over 50 have an annual limit of £10,680 of which £5,340 may be in cash.

Tax rates

Chancellors have to be seen to be earning their keep, so each year's budget produces some tinkering with tax rates, allowances and incentives. Recently there has been a spate of last year's incentives suddenly being relabelled 'vicious avoidance loopholes' that need to be withdrawn. Sometimes impending elections or other political exigencies produce a need for other public reactions as well. As a result, the picture continuously shifts in detail. That is why this section has given a general picture and the overall policies but carefully omitted numbers. To get the latest levels of tax rates, allowances and benefits, telephone any of the 10 largest accountancy firms, all of which will almost certainly have a free leaflet summarizing the current position.

Glossary

acid test: a check in the company's balance sheet to see if it has enough liquid assets to meet its current debts.

Alternative Investment Market: the part of the London Stock Exchange for small companies or ones too young to meet the requirements for full quotation; often abbreviated to Aim.

assets: in a company's balance sheet these are the things it owns or are owed to it; net assets in the balance sheet are defined as capital plus reserves, or total assets minus current liabilities, and deducting the long-term creditors.

authorized share capital: every company has a memorandum and articles of association and these show how many shares it may issue. It is not compelled to issue all of them and many companies keep some in reserve for rights issues, employee incentives and the like (*see also* issued share capital).

bear market: a time of generally falling share prices.

bid: the price at which the managers of unit trusts will buy back the units from investors, compared with the offer at which they sell units; also loosely used for the offer in a takeover.

blue chip: a top-quality company and its shares, derived from the top-value gaming chips used in casinos and poker.

bond: an IOU issued by a borrower to the lender to acknowledge the debt; it normally carries a fixed rate of interest and can be traded (eg gilts, debentures).

bonus issue: another name for a scrip issue; the distribution of shares to existing holders at no cost to them.

broker: *see* stockbroker.

bull market: a period of rising share prices.

call option: the right to buy a share at a set price within the period of the agreement.

capitalization issue: see scrip issue.

common stock: US name for ordinary shares.

consumer price index: a weighted index of a collection of goods chosen by the government to measure the change in average prices and so indicate the rate of inflation. Known commonly as the CPI, it is an alternative to the retail prices index (RPI).

convertible: a class of paper issued by companies (such as loan stock or preference shares) that can be converted into ordinary shares at a pre-set price, and usually on a set date.

coupon: the interest rate on a corporate bond; it comes from the practice in the past of attaching to the certificate a series of coupons that one had to clip off and send to the company to collect the interest.

Crest: an electronic share registry and transfer system operated by the London Stock Exchange, which gets rid of the need for paper certificates.

cum dividend: the share is sold with the entitlement to the newly declared dividend.

dead-cat bounce: a small short-term recovery in a falling stock market, derived from a rather sick metaphor: even a dead cat will bounce slightly if dropped from high enough, but that does not mean it has come back to life.

debenture: a type of corporate bond.

derivative: a generic term to cover something at some stage removed from the direct investment but dependent on it, so it includes options, warrants, futures, swaps, indices, structured debt obligations and deposits, caps, floors, collars, forwards and combinations of these; standardized versions of some (eg futures and options) are traded on exchanges.

disintermediation: cutting out the middleman.

dividend: it is stated as so much per share, so a company declaring a dividend of 12p pays that amount to the holder for every share on issue. The owner of 1,000 shares would get £12, minus tax.

dividend cover: shows what proportion of the company's earnings are being paid to shareholders or, to put it another way, a measure of the number of times a company's net of tax dividend is covered by its net profit.

dividend yield: the amount of dividend per share (usually quoted net of tax) as a percentage of the share price.

equities: another name for ordinary shares.

exceptional items: profits or losses in the company accounts from dealings that are not part of the company's main trading activities, such as the sale of a factory.

ex-dividend: a share being sold soon after a dividend has been declared, with the seller still getting the payment.

flotation: bringing a company to the stock market to get its shares publicly traded.

FTSE100: stock market index covering the 100 companies with the largest market capitalization. Since companies grow or shrink, become fashionable or are suddenly shunned, the constituents of the index change continually. As a result it is an indication of the temper of the market as a whole rather than showing the performance of any specific set of companies.

FTSE All-Share: the aggregation of the FTSE100, FTSE250 and FTSE Small Cap indices; it does not cover all shares on the market.

fundamental analysis: looking at the company behind the share, it involves calculating net asset value and probable future dividends, which may involve economic predictions as well; it is in contrast to technical analysis, which looks only at the changes in share prices.

gearing: in balance sheets, a ratio of a company's borrowings to its equity.

gilts: short for gilt-edged, the usual name for government-issued bonds.

hedging: protecting against a potential liability.

independent financial adviser: somebody who gives independent investment advice to private investors.

insider: somebody with privileged access to information about a company, such as a director; it is illegal to trade in shares on such knowledge.

IPO: initial public offering; US term for flotation.

issued share capital: these are the shares the company has actually sold as opposed to the authorized share capital that it is allowed to sell.

leverage: US name for gearing.

liquidation: the sale of an insolvent company's assets to pay creditors.

liquidity: one meaning is a measure of the market: how easy it is to buy or sell the shares, which is a function of how many shares are available, how many people trade in them and how great the volume of dealings is; another meaning is a measure of how readily an asset can be turned into cash: the more readily, the more liquid it is.

LIBOR: London Inter-Bank Offered Rate, the interest charged by most stable banks lending to each other.

long: owning an investment in anticipation of the price rising; opposite of going short.

market capitalization: the value of a quoted company on the stock market: a simple procedure multiplying the value of each share by the number of shares on issue; so if a company has issued 5 million shares and they are now trading at 125p, the company's market capitalization is £6,250,000.

market correction: a fall in share prices.

members: the shareholders of a company.

MSCI world index: a stock market **index** of shares traded on several markets around the world. It is maintained by **MSCI**, formerly known as Morgan Stanley Capital International.

Nasdaq: National Association of Securities Dealers Automated Quotation system; New York-based electronic stock market with a heavy emphasis on companies using advanced technology.

Nasdaq OMX Europe: London-based trading facility for approximately 800 European blue-chip shares.

net asset value: all the assets of a company minus all its liabilities and capital charges.

Neuer Markt: Frankfurt-based market for shares of smaller, younger companies than are normally admitted to the main stock exchange.

noise trader: someone dealing for the wrong reasons, caught up by the 'noise' in the market and seduced into trades by gossip, fashion and phoney analysis.

nominee account: shares held by an institution or company on behalf of individual shareholders.

offer: the price at which managers of unit trusts sell the units to the public; it is higher than the bid price at which they are prepared to buy them back, and the difference is the spread.

open-ended: an investment vehicle that issues paper in ratio to the amount of investment it receives from the public; unit trusts (called mutual funds in the United States); there is no secondary market in the paper, so buying and selling is only with the management company.

Plus Markets: UK-based stock exchange that evolved from OFEX to rival the London Stock Exchange's junior market, Aim.

pound cost averaging: accumulating a holding by investing the same amount of pounds in the securities at intervals; you get more shares for the money when the price is falling and that reduces the average cost per share.

preferred stock: US name for preference shares.

price/earnings ratio: this compares the current price of the share with the attributable earnings per share. It is the way the market compares expected growth in a company's dividend with the required rate of return of an investor. The formula says the correct price equals the expected current dividend, divided by the required return and expected growth in the company's dividends. So if the dividend now is 10p per share and this is expected to grow by 5 per cent a year, but the current demand is for a return of 8 per cent, the calculation is $10/(0.08 - 0.05)$, which would make the right share price 333p.

put option: the right to sell a share at a set price within the period of the agreement.

registrar: the organization that maintains the record of a company's shares and their ownership; run by specialist registrar companies, most of them owned by major banks.

re-rating: a change of opinion by the stock market: a surge of good news, a series of analysts' reports, the promise of new products and the like may make investors feel the company's prospects are better than the price rises, with a corresponding rise in the price/earnings ratio and fall in the yield, and conversely the other way.

reserves: the non-distributed profits of a company, plus profits from revaluing assets, plus any share premium; this is not money in the bank but is used in the business, though it remains part of the shareholders' funds.

retail prices index: a measure of prices in a set basket of domestic retail goods and services. Known as the RPI, it is generally considered to give a more accurate picture of the cost of living than the alternative, the consumer price index (CPI).

return on capital: measures the efficiency with which the company is using its long-term funds by dividing trading profit (before exceptional items, interest and tax) by the average capital employed over the period (shareholders' funds plus borrowings) and multiplies the result by 100.

return on investments: *see* yield.

rights issue: one way a company raises money is by selling more shares, and sometimes it does this by giving the people who already own its shares the right of first refusal in proportion to the shares they already own.

rule of 20: a way of judging the euphoria or gloom of the market as a whole; it says the price/earnings ratio plus the inflation rate should equal 20.

scrip issue: free issue of shares to existing holders converting corporate reserves into equities – an accounting exercise.

SEATS Plus: a trading system used for Aim stocks and for other shares without enough market-makers to create a competitive market; the computer screen shows any market-makers' prices plus orders from buyers and sellers seeking a counter-party.

sell short: selling shares one does not own in the hope of buying them cheaper in a falling market before delivery is due.

share premium: if the nominal value of a company's share is 20p but it issues them at 50p, the 30p difference is in the books as the share premium account.

shareholders' funds: the assets of a company minus its liabilities; since the shareholders own the business what is left ultimately belongs to them.

short: going short means a dealer is committed to delivering shares he or she does not own; it is done in anticipation of a falling price.

spread: the difference between the buying and selling price of a share or other asset.

stockbroker: a professional dealer in securities who acts as an agent for investors.

straddle: buying simultaneously a buy and a put option in a share with the same exercise price and expiry date; a technique in options trading used by investors who expect volatility in the price of the underlying shares, it widens the break-even point but means they can make money if there is a substantial movement in either direction.

Structured notes: debt securities not backed by mortgages, with cash flow dependent on an index or indices and/or with embedded forwards or options.

support: in chartism it is the level at which falling prices stop or bounce because buyers are being tempted back.

technical analysis: in practice another name for the chartist way of looking at the market; it uses not just the conventional method of having a line to depict price movements, but also 'point and figure' charts.

Tradepoint: a company (itself traded on the Alternative Investment Market) providing an electronic market in shares.

unit trusts: an open-ended investment vehicle (see above).

volatility: the amount of fluctuation in a share price; the more it moves the greater the risk.

warrants: a type of investment allowing the holder to buy paper from the issuer at a fixed price sometime in the future; most are listed on the stock exchange and can be traded like any other investment, prior to their expiry date.

with-profits policy: an insurance cover that guarantees a payment at the end of the set term or on death, but which also adds an annual and a terminal bonus, the size of which depends on the company's profit; that in turn is affected mainly by its investment in shares.

yield: calculated by taking the amount of a dividend as a percentage of the current share price. If the shares stand at 120p (irrespective of what the nominal price might be) a dividend of 12p represents a yield of 10 per cent. If the shares then drop to 100p, the yield will have correspondingly risen to 12 per cent. It is listed in the newspapers as yield and compares directly with what can be had in a bank or building society for the money, but should be higher.

Index